HAUNTED
CENTRAL
NEW YORK

HAUNTED
CENTRAL
NEW YORK

DENNIS WEBSTER

Haunted
America

Published by Haunted America
A Division of The History Press
Charleston, SC
www.historypress.com

First published 2023

Manufactured in the United States

ISBN 9781467153997

Library of Congress Control Number: 2023937155

Notice: The information in this book is true and complete to the best of our knowledge. It is offered without guarantee on the part of the author or The History Press. The author and The History Press disclaim all liability in connection with the use of this book.

This collection of haunted locations is dedicated to the grand dame of paranormal investigations, Bernadette Peck. She has spent over fifty years investigating haunted locations and interacting with ghosts and leading her team, the Ghost Seekers of Central New York. Bernadette hails from an age where technology was nothing more than a 35mm film camera and a tape recorder. An age where the best instruments were the five human senses. Her skillset and gentle, ethical and low-key ghost hunting style have yielded incredible results and influenced paranormal investigators for decades. Bernadette is an American original and belongs among the best spiritual connectors to have walked this planet.

CONTENTS

Foreword, by Bernadette Peck   9
Acknowledgements   11
Author's Note on the Paranormal   13

The Ghost Seekers of Central New York   15
Central New York   19
Haunted Locations   21
   Gerber's 1933 Tavern | *Utica*   21
   1839 Stone House | *Prospect*   25
   Liberty Hall | *Westernville*   27
   Angry Garlic | *Baldwinsville*   29
   Rutger Mansion No. 3 | *Utica*   30
   Brae Loch Inn | *Cazenovia*   37
   Our Cause Tavern | *Verona Beach*   39
   Anchor Light Inn | *Verona Beach*   42
   Oneida Lake House | *Sylvan Beach*   44
   The Stief | *Utica*   46
   Stanley Theatre | *Utica*   49
   Sarah E. Gilbert Boarding House | *Utica*   54
   Masonic Temple | *Utica*   56
   Fort Schuyler Club | *Utica*   59
   Alexander Hamilton Institute | *Clinton*   62
   Capitol Theatre | *Rome*   66

Shoppes at the Finish Line | *Utica* 69
Ilion Little Theatre | *Ilion* 73
Ilion Free Public Library | *Ilion* 78
Overlook Mansion | *Little Falls* 81
Whitestown Town Hall | *Whitesboro* 85
Utica Public Library | *Utica* 87
Colonel Kast House | *Mudville* 91
Episcopal Church | *Herkimer* 95
1884 Suiter Mansion | *Herkimer* 98
Just an Ol' Farm House | *West Winfield* 102
1852 Walcott Family Crypt | *New York Mills* 104
Orchard Hall | *Sauquoit* 106
Gardner Farm Inn | *Troy* 110
Best of the Rest 117
History of Ghost Hunting 121

Bibliography 125
About the Author 127

FOREWORD

I am scared of ghosts. I have been frightened all my life—my first paranormal encounter was with a ghost lady in a red dress with flowing sable hair and a mouth smeared with squid ink lipstick. I was a little girl when she would visit me every night and watch me in my bedroom. She'd stare at me in silence while my heart would be in my throat and my pulse raced, yet I couldn't look away. What did she want with me? What was her message? All my life I have chased the meaning behind her visits. I knew that my life's journey would be trying to discover the meaning of what happens to the soul in our body upon our death. For decades, I was drawn to abandoned mansions, graveyards, crumbling abandoned asylums and all places where ghosts hide in the shadows. I decided in 1999 to share my calling by forming my group, the Ghost Seekers of Central New York. I brought in those who had similar passions as me as we officially embarked on a spiritual safari, which my team has now been on for twenty-four years. So, you may ask, why Central New York? What is it about this area that produces an abundance of haunted locations? I have lived all my life in Central New York, and the majority of my paranormal investigations, ghost seeking and spiritual interactions have taken place in this geographic region. Why is this region so haunted? The geography is first and foremost, as Central New York is abundant with rivers, lakes, streams, ponds and swamps. Spirits can use water as a means of travel and communication. There's something about the rolling hills, deep brown fertile soil, abundance of crisp and cold waterways and wide variety of trees that has drawn and kept humans bound here as

Grand dame of the Paranormal, Bernadette Peck. *Photo by Mike Marrone.*

mortals and lingering forever as ghosts. The blood of patriots and the brave stain the soil, and the multitude of cultures are the band on the multifaceted human floral bouquet that ties the souls to the land. As a lady with many decades of paranormal and spiritual interactions, I am always asked my advice on what it is to be a ghost hunter and what I have learned from my life's work. My advice to those who read this book and wish to embark on their own ghost hunting journey is to believe in yourself and embrace what you don't know. That's the thrill of the paranormal hunt: the discovery and undercovering little slices of souls and interactions with spirits. Have fun, have love, embrace your passion and gather those around you who share the same positive karma. Then, no matter the outcome of your ghost hunting, you shall be successful in mind, body and spirit. Alas, my journey of seeking ghosts shall someday come to my mortal end. What do I want my legacy to be? When I am no longer in my body and my soul has risen to the next experience, I'd like to be remembered as a person who had love and passion for all people alive in this world and those spirits on the other side waiting to embrace me with an eternal hug.

—Bernadette Peck, founder and lead investigator,
Ghost Seekers of Central New York

Acknowledgements

T he author would like to thank those who assisted in the creation of this book: Josh Aust, Jim Barr, Val Barr, Len Bragg, Liz Bridgman, Don Carbone, Tony Carbone, Denise Cavanaugh, Helen Clausen, Irene Crewell, Judi Cusworth, Bobbi Delucia, Steve Grant, John Hughes, Christine Huxtable, Sue Keller, Michelle Klosek, Steven Klosek, Rocco LaDuca, Paranormal Ed Livingston, Judy Mallozzi, Mark Mojave, Susan Nackley Mojave, Diane Nassar, Mike Nassar, Travis Olivera, Dana Nimey-Olney, Joe Ostrander, Victoria Paolozzi, Robert Paquette, Carol Pearo, Bernadette Peck, David Peck, Art Pierce, Gary Puleo, Sharon Puleo, Eileen Ratnour, Randy Ratnour, Maggie Robertson, Mic Robertson, Jeff Rogers, Tiffany Rogers, Chris Sagaas, Jim Skinner, Darcy Stevenson, Kelly Stone, Robert Sullivan, Linda Sullivan Fatata, Darsy Magdalena Sarmiento Delgado-Webster, Mark Webster, Lisa A. della Santina Wilsey, the Westernville Historical Society, the Oneida County History Center, the Landmarks Society of Greater Utica, the Herkimer County Historical Society and all the people associated with the places listed in this book. Without all of them, this book would not exist.

AUTHOR'S NOTE ON THE PARANORMAL

Author, ghost hunter and paranormal investigator Dennis Webster. *Photo by AOisthefuture.*

I have been hunting ghosts with the Ghost Seekers of Central New York for over a decade and have walked many haunted theaters, mansions, graveyards and churches. I started out as a curious writer/author who was a skeptic and grew to realize ghosts are real and interact with the living. People will ask me questions about ghosts. Are they real? What are they? What happens to us in the afterlife? I'm also asked many other questions on what spirits are and what we will experience in the afterlife. Could it be that our souls forever drift after we are gone? Perhaps heaven awaits where we are with loved ones for eternity. Some theories are our souls are reincarnated and placed back into a fresh blank body in the womb. Ghosts might just be humans on the other side of a multiverse who are peeking through the veil at our experience. The truth is I don't know. We will all know eventually when our carbon flesh husks fail and crumble to dust as our spirits rise. Only when we are among the dead will we know the truth. And perhaps at that point I'll come haunt you and whisper in your sleeping ear the truth—but only if you're open-minded enough to believe.

THE GHOST SEEKERS OF CENTRAL NEW YORK

There exists a team of spirit hunters based within the rim of the Mohawk Valley that has over 150 years of combined ghost hunting experience, and that's the Ghost Seekers of Central New York. The team's founder, Bernadette Peck, is a pioneer in the field of paranormal investigations, having been ghost seeking since the 1970s. Her interactions with the dead predate current iterations of ghost hunters by decades, and her experience flows into the members, producing amazing results. The team is rounded out by medium Josh Aust; investigators Len Bragg, Liz Bridgman, Helen Clausen, Paranormal Ed Livingston, David Peck and Mark Webster; and author and paranormal investigator Dennis Webster. The secret to their success is the positive karma, spirituality and love the team members have for one another. Their souls work together as a positive spirit-connecting team that produces unparalleled results. The Ghost Seekers of Central New York start and end every investigation with a prayer of protection but also ask the good spirits to step forth and communicate. The team does not conjure, challenge or attempt to irritate the afterlife souls but embrace them, welcome them and respect their journey. To better understand the karma of the team, please read below their philosophy and advice.

BERNADETTE PECK is the founder and lead investigator and has been a ghost hunter all her life, having had a vision of an entity of a lady in a red dress when she was a child. Her skillset is the ability to see, hear and feel entities as they reach out from the other side. Her calling to the paranormal has been to understand life and what happens to the soul upon our demise.

Her advice is to believe. To pay attention to the little things as a ghost encounter may happen within a small soulful sliver of an earthbound humanistic event.

Ghost Seekers of CNY.

JOSH AUST has been a member of the Ghost Seekers of Central New York for over a decade and brings to the table the ability to see ghosts with his third eye. Josh has the rare triad of paranormal skills in being a medium, a psychic and an empath. Josh has a tech background, so he's able to blend his humanistic five senses with that of ghost gadgetry in order to deliver the perfect earthbound paranormal investigative mix. Josh's advice is to keep smiling and express joy in seeking spirits and do your best to debunk but embrace and enjoy the verified existence of ghosts.

LEONARD BRAGG has been a paranormal investigator most of his life and experienced his first ghost encounter at fourteen years old. He's the team videographer and has captured many ghosts on his trusty shoulder-mounted night vision video camera. Len believes in using your senses as your best ghost hunting tool. His advice is to be ready for anything and believe your senses.

LIZ BRIDGMAN is a sensitive whose psychic skills help communicate with the other side. Liz has the ability to get ghosts to reveal themselves to the mortal plane. She likes to use her skill in conjunction with the spirit box, a device that searches frequencies and communicates. She feels ghosts are people who have passed away yet have a reason to stay behind. Liz's advice is believe in your feelings. If you sense something, speak about it. Every time the Ghost Seekers conduct an investigation, when Liz is in your vicinity, expect the unexpected.

HELEN CLAUSEN was an original member of the Ghost Seekers when it was formed in 1999. Helen passed away but was an active member of the group until her demise. Helen was a gifted medium and paranormal investigator whose style was one of quiet observation, yet spirits were drawn to her. She often found herself in the midst of a spiritual encounter with the grumpiest and darkest of entities. This was due to the strength of her soul and her paranormal abilities. Helen's death has left a hole in the hearts of the seekers, and she is forever a member in spirit.

EDWARD LIVINGSTON is called "Paranormal Ed" and has a gift for capturing ghosts, entities and all manner of paranormal activity on his trusty digital camera. Ed has been ghost hunting most of his life and brings to the team a highly evolved, educated mind with his engineering degree and mathematical application to seeking the dead. Ed feels that ghosts are disembodied spirit energy that are metaphysical remnants of a real-life deceased soul. Ed chases ghosts to obtain answers to the unknown, and his advice to those searching answers to ghosts is to keep seeking and enjoy the journey.

David Peck has been the solid-as-a-rock husband to founder and lead investigator Bernadette Peck since she founded the Ghost Seekers of Central New York. David is a solid seeker behind his video camera and went from a skeptic to a believer, with his scariest event being backed up into a corner by an agitated ghost. His advice to the paranormal enthusiast is to pay attention to your personal experiences.

Mark Webster has been through many investigation as a paranormal ghost hunter, with his spookiest encounter seeing a shadow person in the haunted Brae Loch Inn. His skill is being quiet and observing with his keen eye all manner of paranormal activity. Mark seeks spirits because he is a curious about what they want in our realm. Mark's advice is keep an open mind until you go over all the evidence. He encourages all curious enthusiasts of the paranormal and ghosts to keep hunting.

Dennis Webster has been with the Ghost Seekers for twelve years and started out as an observer and skeptic. He followed the group around for years as a curious author before writing his first paranormal book with leader and founder Bernadette Peck. Dennis is an empath and has been known to have premonition dreams about upcoming investigations. He's the chronicler of the Ghost Seekers, with many books featuring the adventures of the group as they continue to search for the answers to the afterlife. Dennis has theories about spirits and ghosts but always says he will know the truth once he is dead. His advice is to go out and seek ghosts on your own or with friends. It's as easy as getting a digital recorder, a Mel Meter, and sitting in a quiet dark place asking questions.

Darsy Magdalena Sarmiento Delgado-Webster comes to the Ghost Seekers from Colombia. She brings a paranormal international Latina perspective to the team and is a linguist with a skillset of speaking three languages and the ability to distinguish diverse vocalizations. Her quiet observational style has attracted spirits who move toward her soft and alluring aura.

CENTRAL NEW YORK

The area that encapsulates Central New York comprises 3,715 square miles and goes from Little Falls up to Rome, over to Syracuse and up to the town of Trenton. The population of Central New York is roughly 774,000. The area is known for the wide variety of delicious apples and was a critical strategic location during the Revolutionary War. The area has hosted spirits for all time since the Iroquois (Haudenosaunee) were placed on the land by their creator. The area is rich with history, as the blood of patriots was spilled in the American Revolution along with the sweat dripped from the brows of hardworking colonists. Many locations throughout Central New York are haunted with the spirits lingering among the beauty of the hills, trees, rivers and streams.

HAUNTED LOCATIONS

T he following locations have been investigated and visited by the author as well as the Ghost Seekers of Central New York. Some are well known to the public and some will be learned of from this tome.

GERBER'S 1933 TAVERN

UTICA

On the corner across the street from the historic and legendary Mechanic's Hall sits a place where the fried bologna sandwiches and the ice-cold Utica Club draft beer are served with a helping of ghosts, and that is Gerber's 1933 Tavern. Harry Gerber opened the tavern toward the end of Prohibition, and it was speakeasy that hosted many business and professional people. It is a landmark in the annals of historic Utica buildings. Gerber's was purchased by Mark and Susan Nackley Mojave and restored to its current beautiful glory. The ghosts certainly appreciated the love and sweat the couple put into the restoration—especially the opportunity to have living guests. Mark Mojave met with Bernadette, David, Josh and Dennis from the Ghost Seekers of Central New York and talked about his tales of the spooky that occur in the former speakeasy. Mark explained that the structure was built in 1850. He told the seekers about a ghost that hangs

The haunted former speakeasy, Gerber's 1933 Tavern. *Ghost Seekers of CNY.*

out in the Mechanic's Hall building across the street that has followed him into Gerber's. Mark stated that the tavern has other male entities he calls "the boys," and they will throw loaves of bread at staff they consider rude. Mark is a charismatic man and has the gift of paranormal attractant, as the spirits feel comfortable showing themselves to him. The team could sense

The Ghost Seekers on the steps of the haunted Gerber's 1933 Tavern prior to their investigation. *Ghost Seekers of CNY.*

the ghosts in Gerber's 1933 Tavern had a cool spiritual vibe that made the seekers agree to return with the entire team and conduct a paranormal investigation. The team arrived on a hot August day and immediately took a team picture on the side entrance steps before loading all the gear into the tavern.

Mark met us to unlock the building and let us in to begin the investigation and mentioned that his mother had seen the man entity across the street. It was the same one he had seen before, except his mother added a little more detail: this ghost was wearing a hat and a trench coat. There could be a possibility that this ghost would travel to Gerber's, but the team would have to see as they unpacked their gear, held hands and prayed that the friendly ghosts would appear and communicate. The seekers asked Mark Mojave to ghost hunt with the team, as his presence would be certain to gain interaction with the spirits from the other side since they had shown themselves to Mark and were comfortable around his presence. The paranormal hot spot is the bar, as it was the original from during Prohibition, when alcohol was illegal. It was dark in the tavern when the team ponied up to the bar and placed the digital handheld recorder, the gauss meter and the ghost meter on its surface. The team settled in and started to chat with the ghosts. Within seconds, Bernadette got the whiff of a sweet tobacco smell; then the entire group heard a faint voice responding. The ghost meter pegged all the way to the top of its scale and emitted an audible alarm indicating that there may be a ghost present. Dennis heard a cough behind him, and Josh felt there were many spirits in the room. David and Len were filming the event and picked up many orbs and spirit lights circling the room and hovering over the bar. Liz and Josh were able to get the name "Harry" when they asked the entity to tell the team its name. Paranormal Ed and Mark Webster both indicated their equipment and devices had been drained of power. The batteries had been fresh and should have lasted hours, not minutes. The bar chairs that were unoccupied had what sounded like a person rapping on the wooden seats. Josh and Bernadette stated the presence of Harry was close to the group in the bar when Mark Mojave felt something touch his arm. The group was confident that the "boys" were present yet would not reveal their names, as Harry was the ringleader and doing the speaking for his ghost drinking buddies.

The team decided to head down into the basement and left a handheld digital recorder on the bar. Later, after the investigation had concluded, the Ghost Seekers listened to the recording. The recorder had picked up voices, whispers, knocking, a loud bang, a tap on the bar and a whisper. The night concluded with the team holding hands in a circle and praying to Harry and the boys to stay at Gerber's 1933 Tavern. You may ask, dear reader, why would ghosts spend eternity hanging around a bar on the corner? The answer is, of course they would want to spend infinity hanging out at a place where when they were mortals they drank, laughed, ate and had entertaining commensuration with their fellow alcohol-sipping patrons. The next time you are in Utica, stop by the place with the best fried bologna sandwich and the tastiest beverages, sit at the bar at Gerber's 1933 Tavern and perhaps Mark Mojave might entertain you with the true stories of his posse of ghosts and their illustrious otherworldly leader, Harry.

1839 Stone House

PROSPECT

The Stone House is nestled in the middle of the hamlet of Prospect and in proximity to Trenton Falls, which at one time was a major tourist destination and visited by President Theodore Rosevelt. At one time, the area a settlement for refugees coming to the United States from Wales. A stonemason by the name of Jones built the Prospect Stone House in 1839 with nothing but a horse, a cart, his stonecutting tools and his two skilled bare hands. It's an impressive two-story limestone structure that stands in stark contrast to the quant wooden historic homes in Prospect. This home is currently owned and occupied by Dennis and Darsy Webster, so the ghost hunters live in their own haunted house. When Dennis was looking to buy the home, he was told by the previous owners that there was a ghost that would walk the stairs and hang out on the second-floor landing by the bathroom. The previous owner had said that her young son kept saying he saw a ghost standing in the doorway of his room. She also felt drawn to and found solace on the main stairs going up to the second floor. That was her comfort spot she had been

The 1839 Stone House. *Ghost Seekers of CNY.*

drawn toward as she felts spirits on the stairs. Dennis lived in the house alone before getting married and moving in his new wife, Darsy. He had a lot of ghost activity, including waking up in the middle of the night and seeing a ghost standing in the corner of his bedroom.

He made his office the spot where the previous owners had seen the ghost. Dennis was working in this second-floor office and heard someone talking downstairs. There was nobody there when we went and looked. The closet doors in the second floor open on their own, and once Dennis watched as the doorknob turned and the closet door opened. Dennis decided to set up all his equipment in the Stone House and see if he could capture any paranormal activity. The evening started out with an electronic voice phenomenon (EVP) session that he held in the upstairs main bedroom by the fireplace. When he was asking questions, Dennis saw a shadow figure walk past the door. There was a night vision camera at the bottom of the stairs pointing up, and you can hear the audio of Dennis saying he saw a ghost when on camera there appeared a shadow figure walking across the top of the stairs on the landing. Dennis then sat on the stairs to see if the ghost activity the previous owner experienced could be replicated. He placed handheld electromagnetic and gauss meters on the stairs. After a few minutes, the devices started to ring and blat at full capacity. A few days later, Dennis was out front planting stones in the ground. He took photos of his work and later on noticed a ghost standing in the front living room window looking out at him.

When Dennis got married, his wife, Darsy, who is also a ghost hunter and assists the Ghost Seekers of Central New York, had the bathroom door open on her when nobody was home and heard voices at the top of the stairs. Darsy's sister and brother-in-law visited and stayed in the guest bedroom. They said in the morning something was pounding on the wall above their heads. They suggested a priest come and perform an exorcism on the house. The next time they came to visit they stayed in a hotel to have a quiet rest. The ghosts of the 1839 Stone House are curious but gentle and thrilled to have anybody visit who loves the beautiful abode as much as they do.

Ghost looking out the window of the 1839 Stone House. *Ghost Seekers of CNY.*

LIBERTY HALL

WESTERNVILLE

Moved from a dead town, it brought with it the spirits of those who traveled by stagecoach. Liberty Hall is a rare historic building that has had the pleasure of being picked up and moved. The building that is now Liberty Hall and serves as the host for the town of Westernville was at one time located in the village of Delta, New York. Delta was flooded and became a lake, so people and buildings in the village relocated. The current Liberty Hall building was built in Delta in the 1840s and was called the Empire Hotel. It hosted all sorts of entertainment, music, drinking at the bar and foul language that kept women and children at bay from that part of the beautiful two-story structure. The second-floor ballroom hosted dances and many town events. With the creation of Delta Lake, the Empire Hotel would be moved and planted in Westernville, where the ghosts came along for the ride. The Ghost Seekers of Central New York was asked by the town historical society to conduct a paranormal investigation to see if the stories and haunted experiences of the townsfolk could be rooted in reality. The team arrived to investigate on an icy cold February Saturday under moonbeams covered by mist. The seekers conducted their investigation with night vision video cameras, handheld ghost detection devices and the minds of the seekers all in sync. When the team went up to the second-floor ballroom, the investigators heard footsteps on the stage and the sound of the

The moved and replanted spooky Liberty Hall. *Ghost Seekers of CNY.*

Medium Josh Aust channeling spirits on stage at Liberty Hall. *Ghost Seekers of CNY.*

piano keys being played. Bernadette Peck felt a cold chill on her neck when a ghostly voice was recorded saying, "No." Paranormal Ed picked up several pictures on the stage that showed spirit lights swirling across the ballroom floor as if they were conducting a spiritual afterlife dance.

On the first floor, Josh Aust, Mark Webster and Dennis Webster conducted an electronic voice phenomenon (EVP) session within the area of the administrative office and received a paranormal welcome in the form of a ghost that slammed its fist upon the top of a metal box fan that was sitting in the corner. The group wondered if the spirits came along with the hotel or were new ones that feel in love with the structure and decided to hang around after death. Sometimes the Ghost Seekers get answers and other times it's a spiritual mystery. There's no doubt that Liberty Hall is haunted—especially within the ballroom, the piano might just play a ghostly tune for you.

ANGRY GARLIC

BALDWINSVILLE

Fire, brimstone, death and garlic. Food, booze, laughter and commensuration. All exist within the Angry Garlic, where the ghosts with hunger and thirst watch satisfied patrons. The mouthwatering scent of simmering garlic may keep the vampires at bay but attracts ghosts that haunt this world-class restaurant. The Angry Garlic is owned and run by Jeff and Tiffany Rogers. The ghosts came with the building that the couple and close friends renovated. It's common for spirits to become active and increase their connection with the living once their permanent spiritual home becomes disturbed by hammers and nails. The multiple-story structure in which the Angry Garlic resides was built in 1832 and has been the host of deadly fires that claimed the lives of the innocent—yet their ghosts stayed to haunt the heartiest of eaters. Of note are the spirits of a Mr. and Mrs. White who died in one of the fires. The walls of the Angry Garlic are covered with framed black-and-white pictures from the past, and who knows if the entities haunting the place had their mortal images emblazed on the photo paper for all to view?

The dead have no taste at the Angry Garlic. *Ghost Seekers of CNY.*

Author and paranormal investigator Dennis Webster visited the Angry Garlic to taste the food and interview the owners in regards to their ghost stories. This would be in advance of his paranormal investigation. Dennis ate the super delicious and amazing garlic bites, garlic meatballs and garlic boardwalk fries. Jeff and Tiffany sat for a moment and described occurrences and interactions with the spirits, including dishes tossed, chefs scared to cook alone and staff scared to be by themselves in the spooky basement. The Angry Garlic hosted Dennis and his team of paranormal investigators in the fall of 2020, and the evening produced many haunted occurrences. The team sat at the bar in the dark with only the outside streetlights throwing in some scant beams of illumination. Within seconds of asking, the spirits started to announce their presence with the gauss meter and Mel Meters, blasting up to a digital score that assures ghosts are present. The handheld digital recorder got an answer from the other side. An investigator asked the ghosts, "Are you present, Mr. and Mrs. White?" There was a response, "Yes, ma'am." The team was about twenty minutes into the session at the bar when a piece of silverware was thrown in the kitchen, making Dennis and his paranormal investigators jump. Even seasoned ghost hunters can get frightened or startled on an investigation, and the ghosts of the Angry Garlic were ready to announce their presence. The team descended into the basement below the bar and restaurant, where there is storage for dry goods, extra chairs and other epicurean accoutrements. The group felt a presence immediately and turned to see a black mist lingering in a corner. The group went into a middle storage area and heard a male voice out in the other room but couldn't make out what he was trying to say. After twenty minutes of interaction, the entire team felt drained and had to go back upstairs, leaving behind the black mist and male entity in the basement. The last thing picked up was on the digital recorder: a whimper and sob from the other side. There is no doubt the ghosts reside in the Angry Garlic. The next time you dine there on tasty garlic delights, be sure to tip your glass in honor and memory of the spirits who remain.

RUTGER MANSION NO. 3

UTICA

Reputation. Some live up to it. Others never match the hype. The Rutger Mansion No. 3 not only meets its haunted reputation but also blows it out of the stratosphere. The beautiful two-story Greek Revival mansion was designed by architect Philip Hooker and built in 1830. At the time, the location was built on the outskirts of Utica at the end of a muddy road up to the top of a hill overlooking the city. The mansion had many owners, but the most famous was the powerful Republican politician Roscoe Conkling, who was a lawyer and thirty-four years old when he purchased the home in 1863. Roscoe would become the mayor of Utica, the Oneida County District attorney, a congressman and U.S. senator. He turned down the offer to become a justice on the Supreme Court. Roscoe was a tall and powerful man in build and voice who was vain and intelligent. His bedroom

The historic Rutger Mansion No. 3. *Ghost Seekers of CNY.*

on the second floor of the mansion has a tall mirror that he would stand in front of and practice his speeches. Rutger Mansion No. 3 was purchased by the Landmarks Society of Greater Utica in 2008. The society has spent a lot of time and raised funds to restore the mansion to its original beauty. The first floor is stunning, with the second floor a work in progress and the third floor in need of repair and remodeling. The construction has brought out the ghosts, and over the years, multiple ghost hunting teams have investigated. Thousands of people have toured the mansion, and never have the spirits failed to disappoint—they almost always greet the visitors. The Ghost Seekers of Central New York was the first team to investigate the mansion right after the Landmarks Society purchased the building and the most recent with a November 2022 paranormal ghost hunt.

The Ghost Seekers of Central New York arrived at dusk the evening of the investigation and noticed a large owl sitting in the tree directly in front of the mansion. In many Native American legends, the owl is associated with spirits and death. Different tribes have various interpretations of the owl's relation to death. Most believed owls were spirits of the recently deceased. Some Native American tribes saw owls as messengers of the underworld that escort spirits to the world that comes after death. Owls are thought by many to be ghost protectors.

The team entered the mansion, and the members who had not been on the team for the first investigation were obviously excited, as the mansion has a spooky aura that you experience as soon as you cross the threshold. The team gathered in the large room on the first floor and was greeted by Landmarks Society members Diane and Mike Nassar. The Ghost Seekers were represented that night by David Peck, Len Bragg, Josh Aust, Dennis Webster, Mark Webster, Liz Bridgman and Darsy Webster. Lead investigator and founder Bernadette Peck was not there but instructed the team to do a ghost hunt in the kitchen, as she had felt there was something in that location when she did a previous walkthrough. Team members were unpacking their technical gear while Liz, Darsy and Mark walked through the mansion in order to ascertain paranormal hot spots. Diane Nassar from the Landmarks Society was telling David and Dennis about a Facebook post in 2011, when a woman posted she had been in the first-floor library and had seen the ghost of a young lady with curly locks and wearing a blue dress. This turned out to be Eliza, Roscoe Conkling's daughter. After the gear was unpacked, Liz, Darsy and Mark returned, and Darsy said that when she walked into the large formal room on the first floor, she saw a ghost of a young lady with blond curly hair in a blue dress. That this young lady ghost turned her head and looked at Darsy. David, Dennis and Diane stood there stunned, as Darsy had not heard the story and was two floors up when it was discussed. The investigation had not even started, and the spirits were eager for the team to get going so they could communicate.

Liz led the team in the opening prayer, and then Josh, David and Len headed upstairs to the third floor while Liz, Mark, Dennis and Darsy went to the kitchen. The guys on the third floor went to the children's room to the right and set their handheld devices down and a flashlight on each side of the room. The flashlights were turned off, as the seekers will ask a ghost to touch them and turn them on in order to get answers from the afterlife. This methodology has been perfected by years of paranormal investigations. Len had his night vision video camera on his shoulder, and David and Josh started to ask questions. David felt the ghost children were in the room, as he had a similar interaction many years ago in the same room with a little boy ghost who played ball with him. He asked the children in the room to turn on the flashlights and show themselves. Both flashlights immediately illuminated. During this event, Len captured on video a multitude of orbs spinning in the air around Josh. The group then heard footsteps and received a knock upon request. It was pitch black in the room, yet there was enough light emanating through the windows that Josh could see the ghost of a boy standing in the hallway just outside the bedroom. The team in the kitchen sat at the table and started to engage the spirits when the temperature dropped ten degrees in five minutes. Liz could see something moving in the pantry, and all could hear footsteps and a ghost whistling. Darsy saw in her mind the presence of a middle-aged woman in black with her hair up and a stern look. She got the letter *R* sent to her, and Liz connected with the spirit, who said her name was Ruth. Ruth related that she was the head of the kitchen and thus was spending eternity running back and forth between the kitchen and the pantry as if she were still serving her mortal employers. Ruth moved on, and things got quiet, so the team moved to the library, where all seemed quiet until Liz asked for a ghost to make a noise. She got her answer with a loud knock in the doorway of the library. Mark asked if Roscoe was making the noise. Liz asked the spirit to make another noise. The team heard a whisper that sounded like a female voice emanate from the same spot as the knock. The group sat stunned as another knock came from the same spot. Earlier in the evening, before the investigation, Liz had captured ectoplasm rising from the floor in the exact location that the voice and knocks had come from.

The two teams swapped locations in the building, with Len, David and Josh going into the kitchen. David asked Ruth to turn on the flashlight. She accepted the request, and the flashlight on the table lit up with paranormal brilliance. At this time, Mark, Dennis and Liz were up on the third floor in the children's room. When the group asked the child ghost to turn on the flashlight, it came on instantly, but Mark noticed a creepy detail in that the beam of light looked like it had the face of a child in it. Right after that, the group heard footsteps in the hall; then a faint ghost voice said something in a whisper. They then went into the other room, which has a creepy cubbyhole. They crawled inside, and when they started to ask questions, the entrance door started to slam open and closed repeatedly. The Ghost Seekers reunited in the large first-floor sitting room and had an electronic voice phenomenon (EVP) session near the location where Darsy had seen the ghost of Eliza. The team sat, as all were exhausted from the ghosts draining their energy. Len was filming the events from a close distance when all heard a growl. Dennis asked, "Are you happy that

Above: A spirit rises from the floor at the Rutger Mansion No. 3. *Ghost Seekers of CNY.*

Opposite, bottom: The original look of the Rutger Mansion No. 3. *Ghost Seekers of CNY.*

Left: An owl on a branch outside Rutger Mansion No. 3 the night of the ghost hunt. *Courtesy the Landmarks Society of Greater Utica.*

Right: Painting of Roscoe Conkling. *Ghost Seekers of CNY.*

Left: Spirit light lingers inside the creepy crawlspace at the Rutger Mansion No. 3. *Ghost Seekers of CNY.*

Right: Roscoe Conkling's daughter, Eliza, whose ghost walks the mansion. *Ghost Seekers of CNY.*

we are here?" and a perfect "No" was answered by a ghost. After a few seconds, David asked, "Are you the lady in the blue dress?" and the group heard and picked up on the digital recorder a clear "Go!" that came from right behind Len. The team realized they had overstayed their welcome if the ghosts were starting to get grumpy. The closing prayer was held, and the team left the beautiful Rutger No. 3 Mansion.

A few weeks later, Dennis was given a colored painting of Eliza Conkling by Diane Nassar. Dennis borrowed the painting and brought it home to show to Darsy. When he showed her the painting of the young lady, Darsy placed her hand over her mouth, her eyed widened and she said, "Oh, my God, that's the girl I saw." In the painting, Eliza has curly blonde hair and is wearing a blue dress.

BRAE LOCH INN

CAZENOVIA

Traditional Scottish fare and food embrace the visitors to the beautiful Brae Loch Inn. But beware, as this gorgeous destination that is warm and welcoming offers not only delicious Scottish food and cozy rooms but also ghosts. The Brae Loch Inn was started in 1946 by Adam Scotty Brown and his wife, Eva. The original location was in an old farmhouse in Borodino, New York, overlooking Skaneateles Lake, but the family moved their business. The Browns brought their love of food and stellar service to the current location near the banks of Cazenovia Lake in 1950 when they moved the Brae Loch Inn to the William Burr Estate built in 1805. The business has been in the Barr and Brown family ever since. The current hosts and proprietors are Jim and Val Barr. The Ghost Seekers of Central New York were grateful to have permission from the Barrs to come and investigate the Brae Loch Inn in the middle of March 2018 and were greeted with a lion of a snowstorm that engulfed the inn and held the ghosts and investigators within its warmth interior. The Ghost Seekers placed their ghost central near the gift shop on the ground-level floor.

The charming and haunted Brae Loch Inn. *Ghost Seekers of CNY.*

The Brae Loch has rooms for guests to stay in on the second floor and a gorgeous bar and restaurant in the basement area. Val explained how they had gone to Scotland and purchased old church windows, brought them back to the United States and repurposed them into the Brae Loch Inn. The group was excited to get started, as there was paranormal energy in the air. The team included Bernadette, David, Len, Ed, Dennis, Josh and Mark. While the team was setting up, Val was kind enough to have her chef cook haggis, a traditional Scottish dish. Mark and Dennis ate it and raved about the flavor. Val had her staff leave so the team would have the inn all to themselves, but the seekers asked Val to stay. She was comfortable with the ghosts of her inn, and they were comfortable showing themselves to her. She would be used as a human trigger object. The investigation was being carried out on a Monday night when there were no guests staying. Before the investigation, the team did a walkthrough with Val as she discussed areas where her she and her staff and family had experienced ghost interactions. The main interactions occurred within the middle part of the inn—which was the original structure—that includes the gift shop. The rooms that were right overhead included numbers 11, 12 and 13. The Barrs had also experienced ghosts in the basement area by the bar called the Dungeon. As the snow piled up outside, the team held its opening prayer along with Val doing a prayer in the Gaelic Scots language. That was a first in the history of the Ghost Seekers and for sure brought out the spirits. The group began the ghost investigation by breaking up into two teams, with one going into the basement and the other in the upstairs rooms. Val and Dennis stayed at ghost central and watched the monitors live. The task of the watchers is to chronicle anything they see that's paranormal, including orbs, ectoplasm mist, shadow people, entities or anything out of the ordinary. The team encountered activity in room 12, with Josh and Len picking up dips in temperature, chill on their backs and Mel Meter spikes. The team then moved into room 11, where Josh experienced chest pains. Val explained that Scotty Brown had passed away from a heart attack. It was at this point that Len picked up footsteps and knocks from the closet. The team moved downstairs to the billiard room, and Paranormal Ed and Dave knocked and heard a knock in return. Mark saw a shadow person dart from the bottom of the stairs by the bar, and the handheld devices kept spiking in increased magnetism and temperature. There was no doubt that Val's presence, the snow and the quiet delivery of the Ghost Seekers were yielding spectacular results, but the grand finale topped off the paranormal evening with spooky results. The Ghost Seekers decided to hold a séance in the dining hall area referred to as the Dungeon. The team lit a candle and sat it in the middle of a table. There was sage at the ready in case it needed to be lit to chase away unwanted spirits.

The séance was started by Bernadette, who said a prayer to keep dark entities at bay but allow light spirits to approach. The group held hands. A séance puts together the energy of all the participants and can be a powerful tool for breaking the veil between the living and the dead. This practice was popular in the United States during the age of spiritualism in the nineteenth century. The energy is intense, so the team decided to hold the séance for only twenty minutes, but the ghosts came in strength in that short time frame. Everyone heard the scream of a woman from the other side. The team described it as the call of a banshee. Bernadette then saw a shadow person across the room, walking behind the bar and observing from a distance. Josh had his ear touched and felt a ghost whisp blown into it. Mark's hand rattled and vibrated. The interaction was intense, and things picked up when Bernadette witnessed with her third eye a female ghost walking around the perimeter of the séance and stopping at each person, bending down and sniffing them. Could this ghost be the banshee that had screamed? It was at this point that the female ghost stopped at Dennis and put her hands on his bare arms, leaned against his back and rubbed her hands down his arms all the way until his wrists. Bernadette decided to ask her and any other spirits to please step back. Her request worked, as things lightened up and calmed down. A closing prayer was held, and the team disembarked from the Brae Loch Inn, marveling at the haunted beauty, marvelous décor and considerate hosts in the Barr family. It's rare for the Ghost Seekers of Central New York to investigate a perfect paranormal package in a solid haunting in a gorgeous location with warm and loving owners and staff. If you decide to visit, eat and lodge at the Brae Loch Inn, you might just have a visit from one of the ghosts.

Our Cause Tavern

Verona Beach

A simple place of honor and joy hosts loyal spirits who enjoy the revelry of the living. The small restaurant that was once Our Cause Tavern sits by the shores of Oneida Lake in proximity to Verona Beach. The restaurant

Our Cause Tavern. *Ghost Seekers of CNY.*

is no longer operating under the name it had when the Ghost Seekers of Central New York investigated, but the building and the ghosts are still there. At the time of the ghost hunt, Our Cause Tavern was owned by Eileen and Randy Ratnour, who were kind enough to host a paranormal investigation in the spring of 2018. The tavern was built by Lyman Spencer in 1879 and originally called the Forest Home. Before the investigation, the team sat down and shared some food that had been prepared by Randy. As the group dug in, Randy and Eileen spoke of their ghost experiences within the building. Eileen was in the bathroom and had heard a voice ask, "What's taking so long?" She stepped out thinking it was Randy, but he was outside sitting in their car, with the tavern empty. During the remodel of the tavern, the owners kept seeing a shadow person lingering in the kitchen.

One time when Eileen was alone overnight in the building, she had gone to sleep after shutting off the light with the lampshade secured firmly over the lightbulb. When she awoke, the lampshade had been removed and was sitting on the other side of the room on the couch. We decided to go low tech on the investigation, as the tavern was small and there was only a handful of us. We decided to let Randy and Eileen take part in the investigation, which produced amazing evidence within a few hours of ghost hunting. The group started out by sitting at the bar and doing an electronic voice phenomenon (EVP) session. Bernadette asked the original owner, Lyman Spencer, to join the group. It was at this point that the flashlight came on, the gauss meter spiked and Eileen and Josh felt a cold entity leaning on them. Josh was suddenly hot all over when the group heard a ting of a glass on by one of the tables. Paranormal Ed asked, "Is this your home?" and there was a reply—a loud snap from ghostly fingers. The group moved into the kitchen, and when talking to the spirits, owner Randy and Dennis witnessed a small black figure dart across the ceiling as if a ghost bat were flying overhead. The team then followed Mark, David and Len into the back room, where they witnessed a heavy punching bag swaying on its own. The team said nobody touched it, so Mark halted its progress. It then went from being completely still to swaying as if a ghost had punched it. The team was speechless, as it happened right there with everyone watching. The team decided to end the night at the bar one more time. Josh had picked up the presence of a little girl ghost who said her name was Samantha. When the team started to ask her to make her presence known, the unlit flashlight on the bar lit up and the ghost meter that was sitting right next to it lit up and blasted a tone to the peak of its ability. The team pulled out the spirit box and placed it on the bar. This device scans radio frequencies and blurts out random words and phrases. When you are connecting with the spirits, the answers will be intelligent and responsive. Eileen asked if there was a female ghost there, and a soft "Hello" came through the spirit box. After a few minutes, Bernadette asked, "Are you still there?" and the female ghost answered through the spirit box by replying, "Yes." The most startling and amazing piece of evidence was what the team captured on a night vision camera. The group was sitting at the bar in the dark when what looked like a small person with wings flew right past the group. Could it be a fairy? Or a small angel? We don't know what it was other than a beautiful piece of the paranormal caught on film. The team was pleased to announce that Eileen and Randy's experiences were validated and that they operated out of a haunted building. Although it is sad that Our Cause Tavern is no longer in business, rest assured that the ghosts are still there with Samantha ready to greet you with an otherworldly hello.

ANCHOR LIGHT INN
VERONA BEACH

The bar and restaurant is now closed, and the former owners and employees can move on with their lives, but no such luck exists for the spirits trapped within the rafters and studs of the former Anchor Light Inn. The Ghost Seekers of Central New York held an investigation at the former restaurant to see if the rumored ghost of a man killed in the parking lot was hanging around the restaurant. The team was invited by the owners Robert Sullivan and Linda Sullivan Fatata, as they had been having paranormal incidents within the dining room and the kitchen. The Ghost Seekers team for the evening included Bernadette, David, Josh, Len, Dennis, Mark, Ed and Helen Clausen (an original member, now deceased). Robert sat with the team and talked about his cooks having dishes and silverware thrown while working and footsteps and noises occurring when nobody else is in the restaurant. He told the story of a man who many years ago had gotten into an argument with his lady while at the bar. They took their fight outside, where she ran him over with her car in the parking lot and he died on the spot. It was believed that it was his ghost haunting the Anchor Light Inn. The Ghost Seekers would investigate to see if they could connect with this male entity. The group said their opening prayer and split up, with one team going upstairs to the rooms and attic above the restaurant and the rest of the team hanging out at the bar. The attic would prove to be the most haunted spot upstairs, with the team getting answers from the spirits. The group had their handheld ghost hunting devices out along with a digital recorder and night vision video by cameraman Len Bragg. There were a few startling ghost voices picked up that were intelligent responses.

On investigations, the Ghost Seekers encounter residual ghosts and intelligent ghosts. Residual ghosts are entities that are an energy imprint and repeat the same paranormal event at the same time and location for all eternity. Think of a broken record that skips. The intelligent ghost is aware of us being there and responds intelligently to our requests, including responding to questions, throwing things, knocking or appearing in full form. The team felt they were connecting with the man who had been killed in the parking lot. When someone said, "Sorry for the way you died," the digital recorder picked up a male ghost voice answering, "Thank you." Right after that, a seeker asked the ghost to show them he was dead. There was a loud foot stomp on a wooden plank in the attic. Josh, Mark and Len asked

Sad spirits spook the Anchor Light Inn. *Ghost Seekers of CNY.*

the flashlight to illuminate if there were a spirit present, and it did. This coincided with the gauss meter pegging all the way. Then, within seconds, there was knocking behind the team near the window that looked out to the parking lot where the death occurred.

Downstairs by the bar there was plenty of activity, with Dave and Dennis stating how creepy the restaurant looked in the dark. The guys received an electronic voice phenomenon answer that said, "Shhhh." As if the ghost were telling us to be quiet. Helen and Bernadette were sitting at the bar and connected with the ghost of the man who haunts the Anchor Light Inn. Helen had an uneasy feeling right away, as she had become the target of the dead man's ghost rage. The ladies were asking him to show he was there, and he pushed Helen on the shoulders, almost knocking her out of her chair. There was then a thump in the kitchen and the sound of a utensil being thrown. The silverware clanged on the floor, and the team was startled, as there was nobody in there—except, of course, an angry spirit. Helen felt uncomfortable and did something she had never done in her entire paranormal investigative career: she got up and walked out of the building and off of the property. She felt the ghost of the man telling her he did not like her because she reminded her of the woman that killed him. Bernadette followed Helen out the door to be by her side. The team regrouped and said a closing prayer of protection.

Then they stood back and looked at the quant little restaurant, marveling at the sheer amount of paranormal activity that had occurred in only a two-hour ghost hunt. Helen was happy to drive away and put the place in her rearview mirror. Sometimes, individual members become the focus of a ghost, and there's never a rhyme or reason why. Josh, Helen and Bernadette are the team mediums and psychics, and they never know what they will encounter on any given ghost hunt. The sad thing was the team had to leave behind the tormented spirit of a man who expired from a tragic death and is cursed to haunt the Anchor Light Inn for all eternity.

ONEIDA LAKE HOUSE

SYLVAN BEACH

Woe is the anguish of a ghost stuck in his traditions of the past as he haunts the floors of the Oneida Lake House. The haunted structure is built on the banks of the Oneida Lake, which for many years was a shared waterway for the Oneida and Onondaga Indians, who called the lake Tiaoqui, meaning "white water." The Oneidas had fishing villages near the Lake House. Dennis and his paranormal team were invited to conduct a ghost hunt at the Oneida Lake House in the fall of 2020. The house was unoccupied at that time, as the summer season had come to an end. The Oneida Lake House is a beautiful multi-rental home with tourists and vacationers packing the rooms from spring until fall. The history is one of patient care, love and anguish. At one time, the building housed an insane asylum run by Dr. Martin Cavana, who came to Sylvan Beach from Oneida in 1891. He owned and operated the asylum and offered a gold cure he advertised as a solution and cure to any affliction. Dr. Cavana proved to be a powerful and influential man who helped bring a carnival atmosphere to Sylvan Beach and held every public office there was including, president of the Sylvan Beach Association. He was also civic-minded and belonged to many public service clubs, with his most prestigious being the Freemasons. (The doctor was a thirty-second-degree Mason.) Dr. Cavana was married to Sarah Robinson, and their only child, Martin, died in 1894 at seventeen years of age.

The investigation sought to connect with the spirit of Dr. Cavana. The owners, Don and Toby Carbone, were gracious enough to allow the ghost

Oneida Lake House stores slumbering spirits. *Ghost Seekers of CNY.*

hunt in their popular vacation home. Don explained this was one of the first buildings in Sylvan Beach, and it is definitely haunted, as he gets feedback all the time from renters on their experiences. We soon found out the Oneida Lake House is very haunted. The investigators started out on the top floor, where it was a little quiet with not a lot of activity, but footsteps were heard down the hall. The team decided to go to the middle floor to interact with the ghosts. The team sat in one of the bedrooms, and the medium in attendance began to get headaches. They picked up a recording of a ghost whistling. The team went into the book room, and Dr. Cavana made his appearance once the team started to discuss Masonry. There were ladies present, and the Masons are a men-only club, so the ghost of Dr. Cavana did not like it—especially when Dennis knocked on the floor three times and asked the ghost to enter. A distinct growl was picked up coming from the hall just outside the door, followed by a loud thump. Dennis again knocked three times, which is an informal greeting, announcement or request to enter a Masonic temple. There was a distinct reply of three knocks. This interaction served to agitate the spirit of the doctor, as he was soon to break the plane of his existence and announce his presence in a memorable paranormal way.

The group went down to the first-floor living room, and the ladies of the team sat on a couch and were asking Dr. Cavana questions. When they asked him if he didn't like the fact that strong women were talking to him, there was a loud thud. Dennis was standing in the doorway, and a good six feet behind him a wooden kitchen chair was pulled out from the kitchen table and pushed to the floor. The noise broke the dark evening silence, and everyone jumped. Yes, even paranormal investigators get scared. It takes a lot of energy from the other side for a ghost to have the ability to physically touch and move an item, let alone pull out a chair and throw it to the floor. There is no doubt that the doctor was not happy about his current guests and was making his displeasure known. One of the Ghost Seekers of Central New York's theories is that you maintain your personality in the afterlife, and this is the case with Dr. Martin Cavana, as he was an intelligent, strong, hardworking man as a mortal and he certainly acted this way in the Oneida Lake House. The evening ended with the team saying a prayer of protection, happy to get out of the building unscathed. The Oneida Lake House is haunted, and you are certain to encounter the ghost of Dr. Cavana. You may want to approach his spirit with respect and the dignity his life earned—otherwise, you might just get a grumpy paranormal reaction from the other side.

THE STIEF

UTICA

Booze, food, fun and ghosts reside in the warm and entertaining pub, the Stief. Varick Street is a place where there are rows of bars, pubs, restaurants and the F.X. Matt brewery, but there is one that holds down the title of most haunted: the Stiefvater Building. It was built in 1875 by a family who immigrated to Utica from Baden, Germany. The four-floor brick structure housed a butcher shop run by Primus and Johanna Stiefvater that had a slaughterhouse in the back bar area. The wooden blocks from which the meat hooks hung are still suspended in the ceiling. The Steifvaters had six children; one died as a baby in the room right above where the bar is located. The building is now a pub named after the family, the Stief. Owners Michelle and Steven Klosek have lived most of their lives developing their business and running their many bars, including Sickenberger Lane and the Varick,

Burgers, beers and ghosts at the Stief. *Ghost Seekers of CNY.*

all of which have been popular hangouts all year long but especially during Saranac Thursday events and St. Patrick's Day celebrations. The Stief is known for its cold drinks, fun atmosphere and now ghosts. Michelle and Steven have had plenty of paranormal interactions. They have seen a full-body apparition of a man wearing a red plaid shirt whom they feel is John Stiefvater. The middle stall in the ladies' room has plenty of paranormal activity including the door opening and the handle jiggling. People have been at the bar with nobody behind them and felt a push on their shoulders. A girlfriend of a bouncer was standing alone in a corner and had her blouse pulled on from behind. There was nobody there. Employee ghost stories include having witnessed a soda gun in its nesting tray behind the bar being picked up in the air and held there and one was in the freezer alone in the restaurant when the door was slammed into their back with enough force to send them forward, crashing to their hands and knees. This employee fled the Stief and never came back. Michelle and Steven's best ghost event was when they were in the kitchen after closing, making food for themselves and a friend. They had a container of eggs sitting on the counter when the lid flipped open, and a couple eggs were flung out and onto the floor.

The Ghost Seekers of Central New York investigated the Stief on a hot summer day. The group was scaled down with Mark, David, Dennis and Paranormal Ed. Michelle and Steven and their friend Heather Elias were included. The group allowed the owners and Heather to be there for the investigation, as they have a strong bond with the ghosts and the building. They would be used as paranormal human bait to pry forth the spirits to break through to our mortal side and communicate. The group first went to the apartment above the Stief, as Michelle and Steven own the building and lived in the apartment when they first purchased the building. An electronic voice phenomenon (EVP) session was held in one of the bedrooms, and right away there was the sound of a door slamming. A door had been shut by a ghost. There were no open windows and no breeze to shut it. The ghost made its presence known when a few minutes later Heather and Michelle asked the entity to show that it was in the room by touching an investigator. It was at this point that one of the team members was pushed on the shoulder and bolted from the room. It was hard enough of a push that the investigator almost fell out of the chair. The team went back into the Stief and were heading into the ladies' room when they saw a white entity move into a stall. There then was a mysterious and ghostly whistle that echoed out in the bar area. David heard a breathing behind his neck and asked if the ghost wanted us to leave the ladies' room to knock, and there was a reply, so the team stepped out of the bathroom.

Michelle had started to describe John Stiefvater when a group member felt a cold breeze behind them and something touched their neck. The ghost then sidled up to Michelle and Heather, who both were frigid and felt it was John's spirit visiting. The team finished the investigation by sitting at the bar. Everything was dead quiet when suddenly there was clomping of heavy footsteps on the wooden floor in the dining room. An investigator got up from the bar and looked, yet nobody was there. The team decided to end the night and said a closing prayer that included Heather, Michelle and Steven. The team asked the spirits to go about their way and not to follow anybody home. It was a great investigation with exciting haunted interaction. The team left and felt good about everything until Michelle called a few days later. Her daughter had worked through college in the Stief and had never encountered a ghost, yet she had a scary run-in the evening after the Ghost Seekers investigated. The young lady was alone in the kitchen making herself something while waiting for her mother to arrive when she saw the shadow figure of a man in the bar run past her. Seeing a full-bodied apparition scared her, and she ran outside and sat in her car until her mother arrived. The young lady was frightened, so Michelle called to see what the Ghost Seekers could do to ease her fears. Bernadette Peck, founder and lead investigator, had missed the investigation but went immediately to the Stief to sit with Michelle and her daughter to discuss the ghost encounter. Bernadette took the ladies by their hands and explained there was nothing to be scared of now that the ghost of John Stiefvater felt comfortable enough to show himself. The investigation had given his spirit comfort and the confidence to show himself. Bernadette explained to the ladies that often ghosts are misunderstood and they are not to be afraid of, as they are like us but no longer in their physical bodies. Michelle and her daughter felt much better, and Bernadette spoke to the ghost of John Stiefvater, explaining to him that he is welcome to haunt the Stief but must behave himself. There is no doubt that the Stief is a wonderfully haunted pub, with the haunted epicenter being the ladies' bathroom. The Ghost Seekers of Central New York were privileged and honored to investigate a place with cold beer, hot food and warm-hearted owners.

STANLEY THEATRE

UTICA

Applause abounds and pleases the treasures of the past in the ghosts who wander the Mexican baroque beauty of the Stanley Theatre. The theater opened in 1928 and was designed by the award-winning architect Thomas White Lamb. The Stanley opened originally as a movie house, and the décor is marvelous to this day, with the lobby staircase a replica of the one

The grand and haunted Stanley Theatre. *Ghost Seekers of CNY.*

on the *Titanic*. There have been many ghost investigations of the Stanley over the years. This adventure was the third by the Ghost Seekers of Central New York. The team was honored to be invited by Executive Director Lisa A. della Santina Wilsey to conduct a paranormal investigation. Every ghost hunt of the Stanley Theatre has been filled with paranormal activity, and all have produced thrills, scares and proof of a haunting, but the one performed in the winter of 2020 proved to be the scariest of all. That is saying something considering the first investigation yielded a video of a shadow person walking the basement stairway and the second one had a drifting black mist following the investigators up and down stairs and engulfing investigators in the downstairs ladies' room. The Ghost Seekers were led by lead investigator Bernadette Peck, her investigator husband David, medium Josh Aust and investigators Paranormal Ed Livingston, Mark Webster, Liz Bridgman and Dennis Webster. This time, the team brought their most up-to-date equipment, including the Boo Buddy, a little stuffed bear that has ghost detection devices inside its body and can speak to spirits of children.

The Ghost Seekers heard tales from the public that there was a supposed ghost in the back row, but in three investigations, the team was unable to verify that haunted claim. However, the seekers did get a lot of paranormal activity. The group went down into the basement ladies' room to start. Dennis spoke to Bernadette about a dream he had the night before in which he was writing at his table and looked up to see a little girl ghost. She said her name was Mary and darted under the table and was gone. The Ghost Seekers had investigated the Stanley Theatre twice before and never contacted a child ghost or heard any stories from staff or visitors. Psychics had ghost hunted the Stanley and never mentioned a child spirit. Bernadette told Dennis that the group just might encounter a little girl ghost, as the dream could be a dream visit. The team would soon find out as they set sat on the floor of the small sitting room just outside the ladies' bathroom and cut out the lights. It was squid ink blackness where you could not see your hand unless placed in front of a flashlight. Paranormal Ed brought out his Boo Buddy and turned it on. Instantly, the device started to talk as if a spirit was touching it and wanting to take it for a toy. Josh, Bernadette and Liz started to ask questions when suddenly the team heard what sounded like a child whimpering. The sound was about twenty feet away. Bernadette asked, "Is that you, Mary?" and she replied, "Yes." Then Bernadette asked if she would come closer, and she said, "No." Little Mary then went back to whimpering. The team took a picture, and within a cloud of dark mist you can see the ghost of Mary. She then disappeared, but the spooky encounters continued.

Liz and Mark were walking the mezzanine with a digital recorder when Liz asked, "Are you sad you're here?" and received a ghost voice replying, "Yes." David and Ed were walking the tunnel underneath the seats when

Top: Mary the little girl ghost at the Stanley Theatre. *Ghost Seekers of CNY.*

Bottom: Spirit light descending the stairs at the Stanley Theatre. *Ghost Seekers of CNY.*

they saw a shadow person dart away. The group kept getting a strong perfume smell; then it would get bone-chilling cold. When a ghost rubs up against you or attempts to draw energy from the living, you'll get the same chill— the kind that sends goosebump waves across your body. The team went up to the balcony, and team medium Josh was getting chest pains and feeling compelled to sit in a certain chair. The Ghost Seekers later found out from a Stanley staff person that a man had a heart attack there and was taken away by an ambulance and later died. This was a wild amount of paranormal activity even for the Ghost Seekers. Bernadette explained that the chilling cold was falling under a snow moon and that was amplifying the spiritual presence. The team was on the mezzanine when Josh saw the dark entity of a man who was tall, skinny and wearing a wide-brimmed hat standing near a door. The shadow man said nothing and drifted through the wall. It was right after this that David picked up a distinct moan on his handheld video camera.

Dave then caught something moving quick in front of Mark and Liz. The team decided to take a quick break and pause a moment to reflect on the ghost interaction and clear their minds, for the best was saved for the conclusion. The Ghost Seekers of Central New York are a unique band of paranormal investigators, as they are made up of mediums, psychics, sensitives and empaths. The group practices positive karma and a kind and gentle approach to speaking to the dead. The seekers have been successful

Séance held by the Ghost
Seekers of Central New York
on the Stanley mezzanine.
Ghost Seekers of CNY.

on many occasions due to this hippie-style approach. They never conjure, summon or challenge the spirits. They politely ask them to appear.

The Ghost Seekers are students of paranormal history and use an original style of séance that was all the rage during the nineteenth-century rise of spiritualism. The team decided to set up on the mezzanine and asked a Stanley Theatre staff person, Gina Cintron, to sit in with the team. Gina spoke with the team and spent time on the investigation. She had a connection to the ghosts of the Stanley, so we invited her to participate in the séance, as this would help strengthen the energy from the collective. The table had digital recorders, handheld ghost detecting devices and a candle. The group sat around the table and held hands. David Peck did not participate but was instead the cameraman. Bernadette said the opening prayer, and right away, Josh's left arm was blazing hot and his right arm freezing cold. Josh then said he could see something behind Dennis. The ghost behind Dennis breathed on his neck and scratched his arm. Bernadette stated that her hands felt electrified from the spirit energy. Bernadette heard something behind Josh, and the group heard a woman singing right behind Josh. It was at this point that the K2 ghost meter on the tale pegged to the top of its scale. Josh then felt something pushing down on his shoulders. At the height of all this, David's camera battery went from full charge to completely dead. Bernadette decided to end the séance, as the twenty-minute session had drained the energy from everyone present. She said the closing prayer, and the seekers let go of one another's hands and just stared with awe on their faces. Even after decades of ghost hunting, it never gets old and is always exciting when you interact with beings from the other side. The Stanley Theatre is one of the most beautiful and haunted locations that the Ghost Seekers have ever investigated. The next time you attend a show, be on the lookout, as a ghost just might sit in the seat next to you or pass you on the mezzanine, wave and walk through the wall.

Sarah E. Gilbert Boarding House
Utica

A home that hosted travelers, wanderers and those seeking refuge from the wet and the cold holds in its strong walls the ghosts of those too tired to move onto the next plane of existence. Within the city lines of Utica there exists a building that at one time was a boardinghouse for travelers, locals and those in need of a warm meal and a soft bed. Victoria Paolozzi and Denise Cavanaugh asked the Ghost Seekers to conduct a paranormal investigation of the multiple-story brick structure that had stories of being haunted. The brick building was constructed in the early nineteenth century and owned by James and Hannah Plant before they sold it in 1846 to Edward and Grace Evans. The homestead changed owners several times throughout the decades until Sarah E. Gilbert purchased it in 1887. She turned the place into a boardinghouse and had a wide reputation as having a place filled with warm beds, delicious food and a friendly smile. The boardinghouse eventually returned to being a private home and then became the law office for William J. Halpin in 1962.

The Ghost Seekers arrived at the house on a hot June day with all their equipment ready to be set up and deployed. The team placed ghost central in the farthest back room on the other side of the kitchen. The building was going through a renovation, so the team felt the time was perfect to conduct a ghost hunt, as spirits tend to get active when walls are being torn down in the home they haunt. The team gathered together as the sun dropped over the horizon and plunged the building into darkness. The opening prayer of protection was said, and the team headed up to the attic where within minutes the ghost devices were all chiming and alarming to the presence of a ghost. Pictures taken that night show orbs throughout the attic. The main area of the attic haunting was adjacent to the fireplace, which makes sense, as that would have been the location of family events, especially in the cold winters when a fire would warm the collective family. The most haunted spot within the Sarah E. Gilbert Boarding House was the grand staircase close to the front door to the house. The wood panels on the walls match the color and style of the stairwell, which is beautiful handcrafted hardwood. The team medium detected the presence of a young boy ghost who was shy and playful, as he would not tell the team his name and kept darting away. One of the Ghost Seekers snapped a picture during this paranormal interaction, and you can make out the figure of a boy crouched down, holding onto the spindles of the staircase and peering through them. The

Sarah Gilbert Boarding House. *Ghost Seekers of CNY.*

team did not realize they had captured this unnamed boy ghost on film until after the investigation when the team combed through all the audio, video and pictures, looking for evidence to prove a haunting. The Ghost Seekers knew the spirits within the Sarah E. Gilbert Boarding House were happy, as the house itself spurts out positive karma and otherworldly warmth.

MASONIC TEMPLE

UTICA

The integrity of the Masons is bound in tradition and so deep in ethics and brotherhood that the imprinted souls of the Utica Masonic Temple perform their duty in the afterlife. On a dark, windy, wet night of an ink black September evening, the Ghost Seekers of Central New York brought their gear to the temple and engaged in a battle with the spirits of brothers no longer walking our plane of existence. The Masonic Temple in Utica is a grand and solid cornerstone to the early days of the city's development. It was built in 1816 and has had in its history members who were power brokers, advocates and solid brother citizens. The Masons have always been a men-only organization whose tradition goes back to the builders of King Solomon's Temple. To be a brother Mason is a high honor and one held by some of the founding fathers of the United States and former presidents. The Masonic Temple is a modest building from the outside but breathtakingly stunning on the inside with adorned hardwood and marble floors. Its multiple floors are filled with Masonic artifacts, artwork, furniture and records that are a marvel of the brotherhood's history.

The Ghost Seekers of Central New York were invited by the brothers to come and conduct a paranormal investigation. Many of them had seen a male ghost walking the upper floors where the meetings are held, with one brother saying he saw a man that he did not recognize walk into the men's bathroom. He waited a while, and when the man didn't emerge, he went in and there was nobody there. It was then that he realized he had seen a ghost. The Ghost Seekers were represented by Bernadette Peck, David Peck, Dennis Webster, Len Bragg, Mark Webster, Josh Aust, Liz Bridgman and Paranormal Ed Livingston. The team was excited and could feel the energy of the haunt before they even set up their gear. Josh, Liz and Bernadette are the team mediums and psychics, so they walked the entire building and felt the paranormal hot spots would be the upper floors where the pool tables and lounges were, the large ceremonial room and the basement. The team decided to go pure handheld and not run lines to cameras, as the building was too large. David and Len had their shoulder-mounted night vision video cameras, and the rest of the team used handheld digital recorders and ghost meters.

The seekers gathered together and held hands while Bernadette led the prayer of St. Michael as the spectral hunt was about to begin. The team

Brothers of a haunted past at the Utica Masonic Temple. *Ghost Seekers of CNY.*

uses a low-key and gentle approach blended with positive karma to yield results. It tends to be a good approach to get the ghosts to communicate, and this night proved to be active. The investigation started with the team up in the large ceremonial room. There was no Masonic meeting occurring; however, it was quite evident that the male spirits in there didn't appreciate women sitting in the chairs, as Bernadette and Liz both felt the spirits focusing on them and circling around them. There were loud footsteps from a walking ghost picked up on the digital recorder, and when the team was leaving the room, one investigator walked into what was described as a bunch of cobwebs. It was thin strings of ectoplasm smeared across the entrance to the room. It was an odd experience that the Ghost Seekers had never encountered before or since.

People often ask, "Do you get scared on an investigation?" Of course, the Ghost Seekers on occasion get scared but must maintain a professional demeanor even in the face of an angry, upset or malevolent ghost. Josh had sensed that the male ghost that walks the temple was aggravated at the ladies being in the worship room and a few sacred spaces. The Utica Masons had given permission to enter these rooms, and they were not conducting a ceremony, yet a leather apron–wearing ghost Masonic brother wouldn't know that. Bernadette felt he was an old ghost from at least the early twentieth century, so he would be ceremonial and strict within his otherworldly brotherhood. Even ghosts have their rules. The seekers encountered a rare interaction with this ghost: he pierced the paranormal veil and physically contacted a living person. The Ghost Seekers were down in the basement conducting an electronic voice phenomenon session at a table near the furnace when Dennis walked into an adjacent room and discovered a plethora of old Masonic ledgers and books. He carried one out to the table, opened it and was skimming through the rolls that listed brothers from the nineteenth century. The Masonic ghost left Dennis alone, as he knew Dennis was a third-degree Mason. It was acceptable for a fellow brother to touch the sacred ledger, but the entity was not happy when Mark Webster touched it and made that known by reaching from his death realm and clawing his ghost fingernails across the top of Mark's hand. Mark pulled his hand back and said something scratched him really hard. Dennis quickly closed the book, apologized to the agitated ghost and placed it back in its nesting place. The team headed back upstairs to say the closing prayer and end the investigation when Mark placed his hand under a light. The entire team gasped, as there were visible raised claw marks, red and bleeding. The Ghost Seekers held hands, and Bernadette apologized for interrupting the otherworldly slumber of the Masonic Temple ghosts, prayed that they stay in peace and thanked them for communicating. If you ever are privileged enough to be welcomed within the beautiful bosom of the Utica Masonic Temple, please remember to be polite and keep your hands off the artifacts.

Fort Schuyler Club
Utica

Glasses clink to the toast of the present while ghosts of the past wander and watch, jealous of the mortal pleasures at the Fort Schuyler Club in which they can no longer partake. The Fort Schuyler Club was formed in 1883 and moved forward with the purchase of the John C. Hoyt house, where the club meets to this day. The building would shortly have electricity and electric lighting installed, becoming the first building to have these features in Utica. In its history, the club had among its members the wealthiest and most distinguished and powerful men in the area. The Fort Schuyler Club admitted women as members in 1981, and today it is managed by Darcy Stevenson. The building looks modest with its red brick surface and deep green awning entrance, but when you walk inside it transforms to jaw-dropping beauty and splendor.

The Ghost Seekers of Central New York were invited by Darcy to conduct a paranormal investigation and ghost hunt of the club. Nobody had ever investigated the club, and the seekers were honored to be the first team allowed into the gracious beauty. The seekers were represented that night by Bernadette Peck, David Peck, Helen Clausen, Carol Pearo, Paranormal Ed Livingston, Josh Aust, Len Bragg and Dennis Webster. The night began with Darcy walking the team through the entire interior and pointing out the places where ghosts had been seen, felt and heard by staff. The Ghost Seekers ran cables to night vision digital cameras on all three floors and snaked them into the hard drive so the entire hunt could be recorded in the dark. The team gathered, held hands in a circle and bowed heads as Bernadette led a prayer of protection and asked/ the spirits to communicate.

The first place the seekers investigated was the basement area below the kitchen and where the employees had lockers. As soon as the team sat down and started to ask questions, the ghosts interacted, with the ghost meters

Fort Schuyler Club. *Ghost Seekers of CNY.*

pegging all the way and the paranormal scent of brimstone. One of the members had an odd-shaped ectoplasm drifting over their head. When Carol asked, "Are you a member?" there came a knock on the wall toward the locker room, so the Ghost Seekers moved over into that area. The entire team commented that you could hear heavy breathing inside one of the lockers then two of the seekers saw a shadow person dart out of the room. The activity suddenly went quiet in the area. This tends to happen on ghost hunts when out of nowhere you get ghost interaction then nothing. The team decided to take a quick break to collect up to ghost central. This is the area where the team has its equipment, bags and the monitor displaying all the night vision video feeds.

While the group took a quick break, Dennis decided to go up to the third floor to take random digital photos. It was so dark he could not see more than a few inches in front of his face. He used the back servants' stairs and came out into the third floor, where he walked across the hall. Suddenly, he felt an atmospheric change in air temperature and heard crunching under his feet like he was walking on a floor covered with potato chips. He thought this was odd, so he backed up four steps and the crunching stopped. He took one step back; then he went to go forward, and his face hit a wall.

Symbols of unknown origin in the basement of the Fort Schuyler Club. *Ghost Seekers of CNY.*

He took out his flashlight and turned it on and there was a wall in front of him. He went downstairs and told the seekers, who explained it must've been a portal that opened. This is normally a way ghosts travel from one place to another and not a way for mortals to travel, yet Dennis had somehow pierced the veil and entered the realm of the dead. The Ghost Seekers then moved into the kitchen where Len and David picked up footsteps and knocking. The ghost meter spiked around Helen, and Josh explained that it was in the shape of a person. The team had a ghost following them around, yet they couldn't get it to speak its name. Bernadette led the seekers into the first-floor reading room and felt there was a female entity present. When looking back at pictures of this interaction, the team was able to capture a women ghost and a boy ghost sitting next to her reading a book. It's an amazing photo that has the ghosts in color. The Ghost Seekers had before and after pictures showing nothing but chairs, books and a wood panel background.

The team went up to the third floor, where long ago the rooms had hosted overnight guests. Some of the rooms still had beds in them. This area is off-limits to guests and visitors, but Darcy had given permission for the ghost hunt to be conducted up there. Josh, Helen and Bernadette are the team mediums, empaths and psychics, and they felt uneasy and chilled in one room and on fire in another. It was the place where the portal had opened, and the team settled in close proximity. Paranormal Ed has a knack for capturing many orbs, ectoplasm and all sorts of spooky anomalies with his trusty digital camera, and this evening would not disappoint, as Ed snapped a photo of the Ghost Seekers and drifting overhead was a large black mist of ectoplasm. The team was tired and drained of energy, so Bernadette made the decision to end the investigation. The team went back downstairs to ghost central, held hands and said the ending prayer. The Fort Schuyler Club has been deemed haunted and paranormally active by the Ghost Seekers of Central New York. The next time you visit, sit with a book in the library and you might just get a lady ghost ready to snuggle up to you and turn the pages.

ALEXANDER HAMILTON INSTITUTE

CLINTON

The grandeur and glory of the institute holds within its bosom the restless spirits of those who are now among the dead. The village of Clinton, New York, is designated as a Historic Village District by the National Register of Historic Places, and one building in the village that stands out among all the beautiful and historic structures is the 1820 Othniel Williams home, now host to the Alexander Hamilton Institute. The iconic yellow homestead with the red shutters and doors catches the eye of visitors, as the two-hundred-plus-year-old Colonial home looks as good as the day it was constructed. The institute exists for the study of Western civilization and secures liberty by educating America's citizens. The Ghost Seekers of Central New York were invited to investigate the institute by President and CEO Robert Paquette. Before the institute operated out of the building, it was the Alexander Hamilton Inn, a restaurant that offered fine dining. The

Alexander Hamilton Institute. *Ghost Seekers of CNY.*

Ghost Seekers were aware of the hauntings in the building from employees of the restaurant. They had strong paranormal activity in the basement bar area along with the kitchen.

The Ghost Seekers of Central New York would be represented by lead investigator Bernadette Peck, David Peck, Helen Clausen, Liz Bridgman, Dennis Webster, Mark Webster, Paranormal Ed Livingston, Josh Aust and Len Bragg. The group did a walkthrough of the inn before settling on the areas that felt the most paranormal within the first-floor bar, living room, kitchen and the basement bar area. Dennis, David, Mark, Josh and Paranormal Ed investigated the first floor while Bernadette, Helen, Liz and Len went down into the basement. The group gathered for the prayer of protection not knowing at this time that it would be needed, as a fierce and dark interaction would occur in the basement bar. The first-floor team started in the kitchen with a few ticks on the ghost meters but nothing strong, so they moved into the first-floor bar area that came across as neutral, with nothing happening. They moved into the living room and began sensing ghost interaction with Josh, David and Mark asking questions and getting a response with the flashlight turning on and off to commands to the spirits. Paranormal Ed was snapping pictures with his trusty digital camera and was getting orbs and spirit lights and ectoplasm streaks all over the place, but some were large and hovering around David.

Dennis was a little bit back from the group and heard a voice right behind him, turned around and there was nobody there. The team kept asking questions, but things got quiet, and Josh, the medium of the group, said they had moved into another area of the house. The ghosts rallied down to the basement bar where Bernadette, Helen and Liz sat together clutching ghost devices that were chiming, ringing and blasting the announcement and arrival of ghosts who were friendly. Bernadette was given the name Charlene from a female spirit that was present. Len was back filming the session when things turned dark, with the lady ghost being chased away and supplanted by a male spirit that was unhappy with the ladies. Bernadette, Helen and Liz are gifted beyond just being psychics and mediums but were connected and channeling their mental third eye ability gifts in order to view and expose this lone wolf grumpy ghost. Liz had tightness in her chest, and Len heard a voice behind him next to the couch. There was a loud bump, and then the ladies asked the ghost to come closer. With this request there appeared a clutch or large gathering of orbs around the ladies as they stayed sitting at the basement bar. The group saw something move in the dark near the end of the bar. Bernadette gave the ghost permission to take her energy

David Peck filming the paranormal activity has an orb companion. *Ghost Seekers of CNY.*

Ghost Seekers surrounded by spirit lights. *Left to right*: Helen Clausen, Len Bragg, Bernadette Peck, Mark Webster and Liz Bridgman. *Ghost Seekers of CNY.*

in order to manifest. Helen asked the ghost to come forward and show himself. Liz saw it approaching, and the Mel Meter and ghost meter on the bar started blasting to the top allowance on the devices. The ghost began to manifest, and Len now could see it in the darkness as he remained calm and kept his shoulder-mounted night vision video camera steady. Liz asked if the ghost knew what year it was, and the group picked up a "No" in response. The male ghost said he would come closer if Helen and Bernadette would remove their necklaces that had crucifixes on them. He then said he was there for Bernadette, and Helen immediately said, "Bernadette is my friend, and you cannot have her. We will not remove our religious articles so you can go away. Leave now!" The ladies then held hands and said the Our Lord prayer in unison until Len saw the dark shadow ghost figure lurk away.

Dennis was standing at the top of the stairs that led from the basement bar up to the first floor, and when the ladies said the prayer and Len saw the night creature bolt, Dennis felt something pass by him so quick there was a breeze against his neck. The basement team came upstairs to reunite with the entire group, and the looks on their faces told the others they had encountered and battled with a surly spirit. Helen, Bernadette and Liz sat down and were completely drained from the encounter. The told the group what happened, and Josh wanted to go down into the basement to see what he could feel by the bar. Liz and Bernadette went with him, as Helen was the protective spiritual shield and the encounter had drained her so she couldn't go back downstairs. The rest of the group stayed with Helen and waited for the others. It was only fifteen minutes later when they came back up, and Josh had an astonished look on his face. Normally, Josh is solid as limestone and cool as a cucumber, but he had seen and felt enough that he left the bar and came back upstairs. His medium and psychic abilities had his entire body on fire, and his third paranormal eye was seeing multiple spirits down there. Paranormal Ed went down and took some random photos, and upon review after the investigation, he had a dark photo that had three illuminated malevolent and grotesque faces. The Ghost Seekers of Central New York had enough and decided to say a closing prayer, a protection prayer, and asked the spirits to stay there and not follow the team home or attach themselves to any seeker. The team reviewed all the evidence, and watching Len's video of the paranormal battle between Bernadette, Helen and Liz versus the angry ghost was compelling. The team never did get the male ghost to reveal his name or his purpose. The collateral damage and toll the team paid after this investigation was an event that the Ghost Seekers of Central New York would never recover from. This was the last investigation of Helen Clausen, as she passed away shortly after this ghost hunt from heart complications. She was an original member of the Ghost Seekers of Central New York. She and Bernadette Peck had a special bond that was more than just friends but more like sisters or identical twins, as their spiritual connection was unparalleled on paranormal investigations.

CAPITOL THEATRE

ROME

Mortal beings sit in the comfort of their seats without realizing that ghosts are sitting next to them, wandering the aisles and gracing the stage in front of their wide entertained eyes. The Capitol Theatre opened on December 10, 1928, and the architectural style is Art Deco with Moorish influences. The theater is haunted with otherworldly phantasms in the balcony, in the seats and on the stage. The Capitol Theatre was haunted before it even opened when a workman fell from above the stage, plunging from the roof rafters to his death on July 3, 1928. His ghost has long been rumored to be seen walking the stage, sometimes with tools in his haunted hands. There was another death in the theater when a man had a heart attack and died on November 11, 1946. There have been many ghost sightings over the years, with one board member capturing a ghostly man figure standing at the balcony and many patrons encountering things their eyes cannot believe. The Ghost Seekers of Central New York were invited to investigate the theater multiple times by executive director Art Pierce. The investigations yielded some of the best ghost evidence ever caught on video, audio and photography in the more than twenty years the Ghost Seekers of Central New York have been conducting paranormal investigations. Paranormal Ed Livingston stood on the balcony and took pictures of a dark, empty stage. The seekers had a video camera shooting the stage and, in the dark, could clearly see with the night vision that there was nothing on the stage at 7:15 p.m. when you could see a flash from the balcony. Upon review of the picture, you could see what looks like a worker ghost standing on the stage holding something in his hand.

When the Ghost Seekers returned for the latest investigation, investigator Dennis Webster took a photo in the same area at 7:21 p.m., and there is a shadow person standing by the wall only a few feet from the last ghost

Ghosts perform at the gloriously spooky Capitol Theatre. *Ghost Seekers of CNY.*

Left: Ghost on stage at the Capitol Theatre. *Ghost Seekers of CNY.*

Right: Shadow person on stage at the Capitol Theatre. *Ghost Seekers of CNY.*

photo. The evening was filled with many interactions. Bernadette Peck, Josh Aust, David Peck and Dennis were conducting an electronic voice phenomenon session in the front row by the orchestra pit when Bernadette's seat was pushed from behind. Josh was able to use his third eye and picked up the spirit of a blond ballerina in a pink suit dancing across the stage. Earlier in the evening, medium Liz Bridgman had picked up the same ghost dancer but said nothing to see if anybody else would see her. When Liz saw the ballerina, investigator Len Bragg picked up what sounded like a little ballerina music box that had been opened. There were also photos of the seats and orchestra pit that showed spirit lights emanating from within the pit.

It was at this time that the seekers captured on video a ghost getting up out of a seat. Investigator Dennis Webster was walking in the dark across the front row when this occurred. The Ghost Seekers had a video camera with full spectrum and night vision shooting the front row when the ghost is seen fleeing from Dennis's approach. The paranormal activity was strong up in the balcony, where the Ghost Seekers broke up into two teams and went up two different times. The first team to go up comprised David, Josh, Ed and Dennis. The team sat in the seats and asked questions of the spirits. Josh had something hold his hand, and Dennis had something stroke his forearm. Ed was able to capture many spirit lights and orbs on his camera, while the night vision camera captured spirit lights floating around and coming out of the head of David Peck. The other team went later in the balcony and comprised Mark Webster, Liz Bridgman, Len Bragg and Paranormal Ed

Livingston. Liz felt the presence of something up there, so she asked them to come and sit down. Within a few minutes, the seat in between Mark and Liz slammed down and was very loud. Len picked it up on his night vision video camera. It clearly showed that Mark and Liz did not move and had their hands on their laps. The team gathered at the conclusion, with Bernadette saying the closing prayer and thanking the spirits of the Capitol Theatre for paying a visit and letting us know they were there.

SHOPPES AT THE FINISH LINE

UTICA

An industrial accident killed a human body, and the brick and beam Shoppes at the Finishing Line ensnared the leftover spirit. The Shoppes at the Finish Line is known throughout New York State as a spooky spot, as it is listed within the Haunted History Trail, but the origin of the building was based on the world's best textiles. On the current campus in Utica, there were many buildings that manufactured textiles with the founding of Utica Globe Mill in 1847. There was a huge fire that destroyed everything, so the mill was rebuilt and reopened in 1873 and at that time employed 1,100 Uticans. Utica products were considered the bet linens you could purchase and were sold around the world. In 1916, the operations ceased but the remaining buildings were eventually used as a college campus for SUNY and are now beautiful loft apartments. The Shoppes at the Finish Line building was many things, from a pub called Utica Brews to the current use as a retail store of many kinds of furniture. The building is industrial chic inside and features brick and hand-hewed wooden beams on three floors of spooky glory.

The Shoppes has hosted many ghost hunting teams, with all connecting with the male spirit that is said to be that of Conrad Hahn, who died in an industrial accident when it was still operating as a textile mill. Conrad was a mason who was working on the mill's elevator when some young boys allegedly started it. Conrad's leg was snared by the rising elevator, and it pulled his foot and part of his lower leg clean off. The doctors amputated Conrad's leg, but he survived only a few days. The sixty-four-year-old mason died on December 10, 1887. The business was long gone, but the ghost of this tragic death lingered and Conrad still haunts to this day. The Ghost Seekers of Central New York got their chance to investigate when Sue Keller,

Shoppes at the Finish Line. *Ghost Seekers of CNY.*

manager of the Shoppes, contacted Bernadette Peck and asked for a ghost hunt. At that time, the building also hosted the medium and psychic Bobbi Delucia, who is a highly sought after connector to spirits on the other side. Sue had been a ghost hunter and not only investigated the Shoppes building but also worked there and loved it. Bobbi held weekly medium sessions with her clients in her private room on the third floor. The Ghost Seekers asked the two ladies to join them on the investigation, as their souls were connected to the building and the spirits that haunted it. The evening proved to be one of an active paranormal state that solidified the most haunted reputation of the Shoppes and backed up the results of the previous ghost hunting teams.

The Ghost Seekers of Central New York methodology is unique and old-fashioned, going back to the 1970s when Bernadette was a young lady and started her ghost chasing passion. Her philosophy for her team has always been one of karma, positivity, respect and love for the ghosts. She is very selective of her team members; they have to have the right mindset and personality and blend in like a family with the rest of the team. Her style has been proven over decades of fantastic spiritual results that defy logic yet stay on solid paranormal ground. The team had just met Sue and Bobbi, yet their gentle demeanor blended perfectly with the Ghost Seekers. The team held hands, said the protection prayer and embarked on the investigation. The third floor proved to be spooky in the archive area where records were stored. The team picked up footsteps and the voice of a man moaning on digital recorder. A few of the investigators saw something dart behind a row of records; then the ghost meter drained and the battery was dead, even though a fresh one had just been placed in the device. The second floor provided a scary interaction when Bernadette was up there with Helen and saw a hag: a woman ghost dressed in all black with long squid ink hair and crooked fingers. When they tried to engage the hag, she disappeared. The team then picked up the whimpering of a small boy. Bobbi and Sue felt he had been there before and asked him to come closer. Josh had a flashlight but called it a torch, as he felt the spirit was from the nineteenth century. He placed it on the table and said, "If you are a little boy, turn on the torch." The flashlight came on. Bobbi felt his name was Nicholas, so she asked the spirit to turn off the torch if Nicholas was his name. It immediately shut off. This was in proximity to where Bobbi conducted her medium readings, so it was a safe space for the ghost boy. The team all gathered in the furniture area of the second floor to continue, as it was very active. Helen and Bernadette were sitting and being video recorded by Len when they said there was a shadow person standing right behind Len. It was at this point that the shadow person made physical contact, as it placed its chin on Len's shoulder. This rattled the normally steady-as-a-rock Len, as he said he felt the ghost and his body was lit up from the interaction. Mark asked if this was the man who died in the accident, and there was a loud thump, then a knock. Helen then stated that there was an angry man ghost present and asked him to speak. Right away, behind David, there was a loud growl that was picked up on the digital recorder and Len's microphone on his camcorder.

The Ghost Seekers decided to take a break and clear their minds, as they were saving the séance for last. This was conducted on the first floor in the area where the former Utica Brews had tables and chairs for diners and guests. The Ghost Seekers and Sue sat at the table, but Bobbi decided to watch along with Len and David, who were filming the séance. A candle was lit and placed in the center of the table along with some talismans and handheld ghost detecting devices. The group held hands and bowed their heads as Bernadette said the prayer to begin the session. A séance is usually held for only fifteen to twenty minutes, as the energy within the group is intense and people can become drained of their spiritual energy as ghosts attempt to communicate. Helen started out by asking if the grumpy ghost was present and if it was Conrad, who died in the accident many years ago. Seconds after her question, an odd shadow appeared and moved across the table. Everything was dead quiet for five minutes when Bernadette asked if the hag, the witch that she had seen earlier, was there. Upon the conclusion of her query, the lit candle in the middle of the table had the flame act odd, with it spiking several inches upward and flapping side to side even though there was no wind in the building. Dennis asked the spirit why he was so grumpy, and there was no response until Josh stated that the ghost of Conrad was a control freak. Josh's statement sent the surly male entity into enough of a paranormal grump that he pushed the chair Dennis was sitting with such force that it slid a few inches and almost broke the handheld séance chain. Bernadette had enough and decided to end the séance, and nobody objected. The team was exhausted from the active night of ghost hunting. The team said a closing prayer and left, but it would not be the end of the ghost activity. Bernadette and Bobbi said they felt that the little boy ghost Nicholas wanted to say more but most likely fled and remained silent as Conrad was most likely controlling him. The team returned in a week and do an EVP session on the second floor where they had connected with Nicholas. It was a small affair, with Sue Keller, Bobbi Delucia, Josh Aust and Bernadette Peck conducting the session with Dennis Webster acting as the cameraman.

This time, the team brought Paranormal Ed Livingston's Boo Buddy device. This is a small brown and fluffy teddy bear that has the ability to speak if the temperature changes, there are magnetic spikes or if something has touched its fur. It's an amazing ghost hunting tool that helps lure in and make children spirits comfortable. It's a technical trigger object, and the group was ready to put Boo Buddy to work. They also placed a Mel Meter and a ghost meter on the table along with a small flashlight that was turned off. The group started out by asking Nicholas to come forward. Bernadette said for him not to be scared, for they were his friends. Bobbi said that Nicholas had permission to touch anything that was on the table. As soon as she made this statement, the flashlight illuminated and rolled across the table and onto Sue's lap. Sue put the flashlight back, and they continued to talk to Nicholas. Bernadette asked Nicholas if he liked Boo Buddy and reached out and touched the bear's soft paw when the flashlight came on. She then asked if the boy ghost missed earthly hugs and hand holding. If yes, she asked him to turn off the flashlight, and it went out. Josh asked if Nicholas was happy in the afterlife. If yes, he should turn on the light, and it became maximum bright. At this moment, Dennis picked up an orb circling around

Boo Buddy. It became quiet, and the group knew that Nicholas went away, as he was happy and content. That was all they had wanted—for the little boy ghost to not be distressed but happy and playful in the netherworld. The EVP session ended, and everyone was smiling and happy for Nicholas. The Ghost Seekers of Central New York were happy to tell Sue Keller that the Shoppes at the Finish Line was an amazing phantasmagorical haunting with a grumpy Conrad and a playful Nicholas ready to interact with all who are open-minded and spiritual enough to attempt to communicate within the beams and bricks of the former textile mill.

ILION LITTLE THEATRE

ILION

A carriage house that now hosts entertainment and laughter attracts and keeps within its confines ghosts of the past. Next to the large gun manufacturer Remington Arms in Ilion, New York, sits the former Remington family carriage house. The Remington family mansion and the carriage house, or "the stables" as it has been called, were built in 1870 by Philo Remington. A difficult economy forced the Remington family to sell the company in 1888, and the mansion was heavily taxed, so it was razed in 1927 to save on property taxes. The Ilion Little Theatre started in 1924 and eventually placed their base of operations within the stables.

The Ghost Seekers of Central New York were giving a presentation at the Herkimer County Historical Society and were approached by one of the theater members who suggested the group investigate the stables, as they had unexplained occurrences within the theater. The group reached out and were given permission to have a paranormal investigation that would include a public presentation of the evidence. The Ghost Seekers will always discuss the haunted stories with people associated with the places they investigate, so they contacted the president of the Ilion Little Theatre board of directors, Kelly Stone, who would meet members to do a walkthrough of the building. This meeting did not include the team medium Josh Aust and Judi Cusworth, who did not want to know anything of the ghost history. Mediums like to walk into places cold and with a clear mind. The night of the walkthrough featured Bernadette Peck, David Peck, Dennis Webster and Len Bragg. The walkthrough was amazing,

Spirits of the stage at the Ilion Little Theatre. *Ghost Seekers of CNY.*

as the ghost detection devices were singing their paranormal tune while Kelly talked about the male entity they lovingly called George. He was playful and mischievous, as he'd take and hide hand tools like hammers; screwdrivers and cellphones would come up missing only to be found days later in other parts of the building. It wasn't an official ghost hunt, yet Len picked up activity on his video camera and Dennis photographed orbs and spirit lights of all sizes and colors in every room. The seekers knew that the place was haunted, but the final verification would be on the official investigation that took place three weeks later on a chilly November evening. The walkthrough identified paranormal hot spots, including the front row of seats, the stage and the upstairs prop storage area.

The Ghost Seekers arrived, and the theater looked ominous, as there was a full winter moon whose strong beams of illumination flickered off the dark green trim of the wooden accents of the brick building. It was snowy, and

Helen Clausen and Bernadette Peck performing an electronic voice phenomenon (EVP) session at the Ilion Little Theatre. *Ghost Seekers of CNY.*

A swarm of orbs and spirit lights surround Paranormal Ed Livingston on the stage at the Ilion Little Theatre. *Ghost Seekers of CNY.*

there were icicles on the roof and hanging down over the windows. The Ilion Little Theatre was saying "welcome" as the Ghost Seekers carried in all their gear and placed it in the kitchen area, which would be the ghost center where all gear and monitors was located. The team that night was made up of Bernadette Peck, David Peck, Helen Clausen, Len Bragg, Paranormal Ed Livingston, Judi Cusworth, Joe Ostrander and Dennis Webster. The opening prayer was said, asking the good spirits like George to come forward and communicate, but any bad spirits were not welcome to crash the ghost hunting party. The lights were shut off, plunging the theater and the human guests into complete darkness, with only their flashlights to illuminate their path. The team decided to go up to the second-floor prop storage area when Len heard and picked up on his camera footsteps going up the wooden stairs. The team settled down among the stage props, and Judi picked up the presence of a male ghost. There were sounds of loud tapping and footsteps, and just outside their view in the pitch darkness came an insidious breath. The ghost meters spiked, and Paranormal Ed was getting massive orbs— many all around the team—as he snapped digital photos. The Ghost Seekers moved down to the stage and had a few odd yet thrilling and unexplained paranormal events.

Helen and Bernadette were sitting in chairs on the stage and having an electronic voice phenomenon (EVP) session where they were asking the spirits to answer their earthbound human carbon husk questions. While they were conducting their ghost query, David and Joe both saw a shadow person dart across the stage. Then Len and Dennis spotted a shadow person sitting in the second row. There was a clear voice that said, "That's awesome"—it was high pitched and sounded like Mickey Mouse. Bernadette said, "Helen, what the heck? Why are you talking in that high-pitch voice?" Helen responded, "I didn't say anything, Bernie." This ghost voice from the other side was picked up clearly on the digital recorders, but there was another voice to come. The Ilion Little Theatre has stage props all over the place and had an old rotary phone sitting on a table. Paranormal Ed and Judi approached the phone, with Ed saying, "I'm going to pick this phone up and break on through to the other side." Judi teasingly said, "Don't do it, Ed." Paranormal Ed picked up the receiver and said, "Hello," and a clear answer came back, "Hello," It was a man's voice but with a British accent. Ed was stunned and turned the phone around; not only was it not plugged in, but it was only a shell, as the inner electronics had been gutted as well.

The Ghost Seekers decided to take a fifteen-minute break from the action in order to recharge their mental batteries. Everyone rallied back to ghost central, and Dennis went by the stage to look at the toolbox and tools he had set up earlier as trigger objects. George the ghost had a reputation of moving and taking tools, so Dennis opened up the theater toolbox and set out a hammer and a couple screwdrivers. When he looked back at the tools, the Phillips head screwdriver had been picked up and moved. The Ghost Seekers had not been anywhere near the toolbox. Dennis went and told the team, and everyone was excited. Len went into the stage room by himself to take a picture. Everyone was having casual conversation when Len came bolting out with a look of disbelief on his face. Len is a solid and professional ghost hunter who never gets rattled in any interaction with the spirits, yet he had a physical encounter with an entity. While Len was taking a picture of the toolbox, a ghost leaned over his shoulder and placed its hands on his arms. The unexpected interaction prompted him to go back to be among his fellow ghost seekers. David got up to take a look, and the large double wooden entry doors slammed in his face. There was no doubt George was present and playing with the team.

The Ghost Seekers decided to perform a séance on the stage. The Ghost Seekers perform their séances in the old style from the early days of spiritualism and always get results, as they hold hands in unison to create a human energy bond. As soon as the séance started, the team picked up a voice saying, "Did you hear about me?" Then whispers were heard as the ghost was walking around the perimeter of the table knocking randomly, and then there was the smell of rose and a distinct, loud hiccup. Things were quiet for several minutes, and then the candle flame pointed right at Len, even though there was no breeze or wind in the theater. Len mentioned he smelled bandages. Len spent his career as a psychiatric nurse and knows the smells of medical operations. As soon as Len mentioned the scent, a loud huff or breath was heard by the entire team. Helen observed the candle slide on the table then Bernadette mentioned the table had moved. The entire group then heard creaking of boards as if someone were walking across the stage. The Ghost Seekers were exhausted, so Bernadette ended the séance. The team had smiles on their faces as they picked up their gear and said the closing prayer. They proved that not only is George the ghost real, but he also lived up to his playful reputation. The Ilion Little Theatre is a wonderland of paranormal activity, but one can't blame George, as the building is spectacular inside and out and always filled with actors and actresses who love to perform for their mortal and ghost audience.

ILION FREE PUBLIC LIBRARY

ILION

Librarians have a soul connection to the place where their calling had them commit their careers and love to the education of the public. Books have a grip on humanity, as we are compelled to chronicle, write and read, which separates humans from all other forms of animals on planet earth. The Ghost Seekers of Central New York have investigated libraries in the past, and they are always active. What could be the reason? The team felt it was the love connection people have with literature and books. The team was contacted by Ilion Free Public Library director Travis Olivera and asked to conduct a paranormal investigation of the library. The library land was purchased by philanthropist Clarence W. Seamons, who was the founder of the Remington Typewriter Company. The Roman-style building was designed by architect George P. Chappell and opened in 1893. Bernadette Peck, lead investigator and founder, spoke to Travis and asked him what activity he had experienced in the library and he said none that he knew of—but the building was of an interesting architectural design, and Travis was a fan of the seekers and thought it would be cool to have them come investigate the library. Bernadette consulted her team, and they unanimously decided it would be worth it to see if they could glean some paranormal twinkles from within the walls of the library or get skunked in the attempt. The thrill of the unknown compelled the seekers to take Travis's challenge to ghost hunt and see if anything was hiding in the shadows. The Ghost Seekers decided to go strictly handheld video cameras and ghost detection devices, as the library was small, and the team would be limited to a few members: Bernadette Peck, David Peck, Joe Ostrander, Len Bragg and Dennis Webster.

The group of Len, Josh and Bernadette headed up into the second-floor loft area, where Josh felt compelled to go, as he is the team medium and has a paranormal bloodhound nose that rarely fails to capture a ghost. Things started out silent for a while before Bernadette and Josh commented on the typewriters that were up there. Josh went over and placed his hands on one, and his entire body lit up. He felt there was something about the typewriters up there, and Josh didn't know the founder of the library had owned a typewriter company. Josh sat back down with Bernadette as they started to sense there was a lady entity watching them. Could it be a past librarian? They got a name: Mary Ann. Josh then said he could see the lady with his third eye. She was a shy and quiet lady in her middle age of

Books, spirits and haunts at the Ilion Free Public Library. *Ghost Seekers of CNY.*

life. While this was occurring, the other team of David, Joe and Dennis went to the basement. They sat in an area where there were tables and chairs. After a few quiet moments, Joe saw a shadow person off to his right. The ghost meters started to go off and spike right next to Joe. There was something about him that was attracting the spirits. The team then heard and recorded on the digital recorder footsteps that echoed off the concrete basement walls, yet looking with their squinted eyes in the dim they could see no earthbound person walking. It was a ghost strolling. David asked for the spirit to knock, and there was a loud one just behind the team. It went sterile for a while before the group all saw something white whoosh right past. It startled everyone. David then asked, "Do you want to talk to us?" The group heard a "No" in response. This was picked up by the handheld digital recorder. The teams ended their first session and reunited upstairs, as a break in the spiritual safari was a mental must.

Josh, David and Dennis went for round two in the basement as the action was heating up down there, and the team medium wanted to delve right into the paranormal maelstrom. They decided to sit in the corner near where the earlier activity had occurred. Dave was filming with his portable night

Orbs abound within the haunted books of the Ilion Free Public Library. *Ghost Seekers of CNY.*

vision video camera. Other than that, the team had a small digital recorder, a ghost meter and a small flashlight. Within seconds, David felt there was something standing behind him, and then everyone heard loud breathing. Josh and Dennis both had the hairs on their arms standing on end, as the ghost was still standing behind David. The ghost was not defined enough to tell if it was a man or a woman. Josh said, "If you are a man, turn on the flashlight." It didn't respond. He then said, "If you are a woman, turn on the flashlight," and it lit bright. David added, "If you really are a lady ghost, step away and let the light go off." It turned off. Josh waited a minute and said, "If you are Mary Ann, turn on the flashlight," and it came back on brighter than before. Mary Ann was able to tell the group she had been an employee in the library and that she stayed in the library because she was happy being forever in a place she had loved. It started to get ice cold, and the seekers' breath emitted mist that drifted over the beam of the lit flashlight. Josh then heard a lady ghost whisper in his ear. Everything then went quiet; the group felt Mary Ann got her message across and decided to go back to her solitary library afterlife of infinity books. The Ghost Seekers reunited upstairs, and the library director returned to see how things went. The team began telling

Travis all about Mary Ann and the details of the evening. He asked Josh to describe what she looked like. Travis left for a moment and came back with old books that had library employees within, and after a few minutes, he was able to find an old employee by the name of Mary Ann and showed the team the picture. It was the lady Josh had seen and described. The Ilion Free Public Library is haunted by a former employee who is happy in her bookish afterlife. Just don't ask her to find your favorite tome, as she may just haunt your selection.

OVERLOOK MANSION

LITTLE FALLS

Spirits overflow within the confines of the large Victorian-era Overlook Mansion, nestled along a picturesque, steep hillside. To see the exterior of the Overlook makes one compare it to spooky movies and a haunted mansion right out of the cartoon *Scooby Doo*. The Overlook Mansion was built in 1889 by David Burrell, who had made his fortune inventing farm machinery, including advanced machines for milking cows. He hired renowned Syracuse architect Archimedes Russell, who delivered a jaw-dropping beauty of stone and mortar sure to attract, host and keep ghosts within its Victorian bosom. The mansion included a second-floor bedroom that featured a balcony, as Burrell had a young daughter who suffered from tuberculosis and used the balcony as a way to get fresh air to ease her suffering. For over one hundred years, the Overlook was a private residence, and it hosted a tragedy in 1978. At that time, the Overlook Mansion was owned and lived in by the Billing family. The Billings had their own biological children but also had adopted two boys and two girls from the Crow Indian reservation in Montana. Life was difficult for the adopted children, and the boys, Bobby, thirteen, and Tyler, eleven, decided to run away from Little Falls to return to their Native American homeland. The boys were only able to get to the railroad tracks, where a train hit and killed them. One of their adopted siblings, Chris Billing, directed a documentary called *Lost Sparrow* in which he chronicles the difficulties inside the Overlook. The boys were buried in a local cemetery but were exhumed in 2009 and returned to their reservation in Montana. Their uncle, Pat Stands Over Bull, said that the Crow belief is that a spirit never

The grand and beautifully haunted Overlook Mansion. *Ghost Seekers of CNY.*

rests when buried some place in a faraway land. These events and others led the Ghost Seekers of Central New York to enter and investigate a place that had never hosted a paranormal hunt. The Overlook Mansion proprietors, Mic and Maggie Robertson, had met lead investigator and founder of the Ghost Seekers Bernadette Peck and author and paranormal investigator Dennis Webster at a book signing event at the mansion and asked if Bernadette would bring her team to investigate, as they and their employees had encountered ghost events on a regular basis.

The mansion was alluring and spooky, and of course, the investigation was agreed on. The Ghost Seekers arrived on a frigid and cold January Saturday where the snow had piled so high that the investigators barely made the drive up the steep and slick hillside. The Overlook Mansion, with its dark brown stone façade, stood out stark against the winter snow. The team all got out of their cars and were in awe of the beautiful Victorian mansion. The seekers team investigating were Bernadette Peck, David Peck, Len Bragg, Paranormal Ed Livingston, Helen Clausen, Dennis Webster, Josh Aust, Carol Pearo and Joe Ostrander. The team was inside setting up their equipment when a paranormal event happened before the investigation began. Bernadette, Helen and Carol saw a shadow person on the second floor and heard footsteps. Dennis Webster was standing at the front desk jotting notes in his journal when a book flew off a shelf and hit him in the chest. He bent down, picked up the book and saw that it was a book of prayers. Paranormal Ed and Joe were setting up in the basement and smelled a strong odor of sulfur. David and Len felt woozy in the kitchen. Josh was in the dining room, and he felt the presence of a child and his ghost meter pegged to the top. The team invited Jim, the caretaker of the Overlook, as he lived alone in one of the second-floor rooms and had described hearing voices and dishes clinking in the kitchen. He would go down and nobody would be there. He said he heard constant footsteps and talking even though he was all by himself in the mansion and the doors for entry had been locked. Mic and Maggie lived with their family in the separate carriage house building. The Ghost Seekers gathered in a circle, held hands and said the opening prayer of protection.

The investigation lasted only a few hours, but the ghost activity started immediately and didn't let up until the completion of the spiritual

The Ghost Seekers channeling spirits as orbs abound. *Left to right*: Paranormal Ed Livingston, Helen Clausen and Len Bragg. *Ghost Seekers of CNY*.

connection. In the basement, there was a ghost afraid to approach and cowered from the team in the back corner. Everyone felt on pins and needles as the energy was firing everyone's aura to full blaze. Investigators were touched on the arm, and knocks were given in reply to questions. The Ghost Seekers went up to the first floor and sat at the large table in the formal dining room. Everyone heard footsteps and talking that sounded like a child. Len took out his Indian flute and played a tune. The music made everyone emotional as we all thought of the spirits of the tragically dead Crow Indian boys. The song ended, and all the handheld ghost devices on the table lit up; then a strong perfume odor hit everyone's nostrils. The Ghost Seekers had to take a few minutes' break to gather their energy before deploying to the kitchen. The group felt there was a portal in there, and that would explain the constant talking Jim the caretaker heard. A shadow person was seen, and a ghost made a loud "huff" behind the team. Helen was pushed from behind, so the team felt it was time to move on.

Up on the second floor, the team went into Jim the caretaker's apartment, where the voices of certain team members became weird in tone and cameras and gear were shutting off on their own. The most haunted location was the second-floor bedroom where Burrell's daughter lived. The young lady had suffered with tuberculosis. Investigators were sitting on the bed when the rem pod went full blast and a ghost was seen moving in the doorway. When a team member asked, "Are you the daughter of David Burrell?" the bed shook. The paranormal activity continued with Josh seeing a child entity fleeing into a closet, Bernadette felt heaviness in her chest in the TB room and Dennis and Ed had flashlights in their pockets going on and off. Bernadette gathered her team downstairs and called it a night as the constant connection with spirits from the other side had drained the entire team of energy. Upon review of the evidence, the Ghost Seekers of Central New York captured on a digital recorder, voices, knocking, footsteps, huffing and odd wooden cracking sounds. The night vision video captured numerous orbs and spirit lights floating around all the investigators and in all rooms that had been filmed. Several fantastic photos captured ghosts, including a face in the dining room mirror, a ghost looking in a second-floor window, a huge orb in the TB room and a large smudge ink ectoplasm in the second-floor bathroom. The Ghost Seekers consider the Overlook Hotel one of the most haunted places they have ever investigated.

WHITESTOWN TOWN HALL

WHITESBORO

The second floor of the Whitestown Town Hall has secured trapdoors that at one time were used to execute murderers in neck-cracking justice. The two-story brick structure was built in 1807 and was originally called Liberty Hall. It now houses the village courthouse on the first floor and the historic society on the second floor. The town hall was placed on the National Register of Historic Places in 1973. The Ghost Seekers of Central New York were invited to investigate the town hall by village clerk Dana Nimey-Olney and town historian Judy Mallozzi. The team included guest investigator and multimedia author, writer and radio show host Rocco LaDuca. The town hall had long ago been the Oneida County Courthouse before it was moved to Utica. At one time, the house next door to the town hall had been the jail. When you walk on the hardwood floors up on the second floor, you can see where the trapdoors had been located. When a criminal was to be hanged, they stood on that trapdoor, the hangman pulled a lever, the

Ghosts of hanged criminals haunt the Whitestown Town Hall. *Ghost Seekers of CNY.*

trapdoor opened and the criminal plummeted through the opening until the rope became taut and the offender's neck snapped, killing them instantly. Tragic and sudden death can leave a spirit trapped at the site of their demise to spend eternity in eternal spiritual torment. The room now hosts historical items and replicas of past village homes. Whitesboro has a long history, having been settled back in 1784.

The Ghost Seekers could sense the spirits in the town hall. It was not a large space, but ghosts don't worry about afterlife elbow room. The team stayed together for the entire investigation. The opening prayer was said, and the group sat among the town historical items and immediately saw a ghost standing in a doorway to one of the rooms. The team tried to get the entity to come closer, but it disappeared as quick as it appeared. Handheld ghost detection devices were placed on the wooden floor where the trapdoors for the hangings had been, and the devices started to light up as if the spirits of the doomed were lingering on the spot of their death. The back corner room had orbs and spirit lights flying around as the team settled in and placed a flashlight on the floor. The Ghost Seekers asked to light up the flashlight if there was an entity present and on cue it illuminated to its maximum brilliance. The team could hear something walking out in the main room, but when they checked there was nobody there. Photographs revealed strange lights and ectoplasm like a sheer white mist drifting across the room. Dana and Judy asked the Ghost Seekers off Central New York to come back and perform a public reveal of the evidence. A nice crowd gathered that night as the team played electronic voice phenomenon that had been captured on handheld digital recorders. The photos were displayed, and the seekers interacted with the crowd. Whenever the seekers appear before the public to discuss ghosts, they always have a spooky story from an audience member.

That night, the team heard the most amazing spirit encounter of their paranormal investigative career. A well-dressed elderly couple sat in the back during the presentation and said nothing until the event was over and everyone had left. They approached Bernadette Peck and her seekers and proceeded to tell them they ran a funeral parlor long ago and that they had never believed in ghosts until one night they had a dear friend pass away. They went to their funeral parlor and awaited the arrival of the body of their friend. They said that when they were alone with their friend in the basement of the funeral parlor, they decided to say a prayer over the body. Then the spirit of the deceased rose up out of the body and floated through the ceiling. The Ghost Seekers were appreciative of the story, as the couple became emotional telling it, and Bernadette held their hands and reassured them it was OK to believe in ghosts. That story was the cherry on top of the paranormal event that was the investigation of the Whitestown Town Hall, a place where the souls of the hanged stay around awaiting their next otherworldly judgment.

Utica Public Library

Utica

Ghosts browse books at the Utica Public Library. What is it about libraries that attract ghosts? Could it be the fondness of learning? The Utica Public Library is a five-story building designed by Arthur Jackson in a Neoclassical style that was built in 1903. The New Haven brick library on its limestone foundation is known for its beautiful multilevel internal glass floors, where the majority of the books are nestled. It's on the National Register of Historic Places and is the crown jewel of historic buildings in the city of Utica. The Ghost Seekers of Central New York were invited to investigate by library director Chris Sagaas. The seekers conducted two investigations over the

Check out tomes and spirits at the Utica Public Library. *Ghost Seekers of CNY.*

Left: Spirit lights in the archway of the Utica Public Library. *Ghost Seekers of CNY.*

Below: Odd paranormal event caught on camera at the Utica Public Library. *Ghost Seekers of CNY.*

Opposite: Ruby's ghost attractant plant. *Ghost Seekers of CNY.*

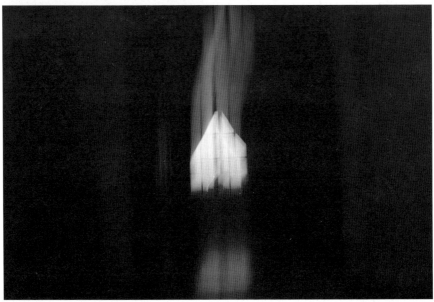

course of a year and received similar results to verify the haunted claims of the library staff. The Ghost Seekers had a pre-investigation walk around by the facilities led by employee John Hammond, who spent many hours alone throughout the library and had several run-ins with a ghost he theorized had been a previous maintenance man named Patrick who had passed and now lived his eternity walking the beloved library. John showed the team the basement area where his office is located. The public is not allowed in this area. He said that he constantly hears footsteps and keys jingling, as Patrick always carried a large ring of keys on his belt and library employees

could hear him coming a mile away. John also showed the investigators the area on the second floor near a conference room where he encounters paranormal activity. He is often alone in the library and hears loud steps on the wooden floor and more than once has seen the figure of a man standing there watching him. Up in the glass floor book area is a potted plant that was adored by a former library employee named Ruby. Everyone refers to the plant as Thanos, and they have seen the spirit of Ruby hanging by the plant. The first investigation found ghosts in the exact spots that John pointed out. The Ghost Seekers were in the basement and heard footsteps walking past the maintenance offices, whistling and keys jingling. It was so dark you could not see more than a few inches from your face. A flashlight was illuminated in the location of the footsteps, and nobody was there.

Later on, Dennis Webster listened to the digital recorder, and the ghost footsteps, jingling keys and whistling were all captured. The Ghost Seekers were up by Ruby's plant when they had a creepy encounter. On the walkthrough, ghost detection handheld devices were waved around and near the plant with no response, yet while the investigation was live the devices all lit up and chimed strong and loud to announce the presence of an entity. While standing by the plant, an investigator was looking down into the area where John had encountered the walking ghost that may have been Patrick when they saw a ghost standing there looking up at the team. When it realized it had been spotted, the shadow figure darted to the left and disappeared. A few quick photographs were taken, and a large orb was in the exact spot where Patrick had darted. The Ghost Seekers confirmed the haunted spots, but on the return investigation, they would get evidence not only in the same locations but also in an area not known to have had ghost sightings. The Ghost Seekers were represented by David Peck, Josh Aust, Len Bragg and Paranormal Ed Livingston. Paranormal Ed has a magic touch with his digital camera, as ghosts feel comfortable allowing themselves to be captured by the heart-of-gold investigator Ed. He snapped pictures showing spirit lights and orbs, but the strangest anomaly was a paranormal smear across one of the library windows. The photo defies explanation, and the seekers have deemed it paranormal but can't explain what it is or what message the spirits were trying to send. The team again recorded high EMF spikes by Ruby's plant. There are no wires or artificial devices to place energy at the plant. Len recorded in the gallery a voice from the other side saying, "Yeah," when Len had asked if there was a ghost present.

The Ghost Seekers found the best ghost evidence of the evening in the downstairs children's room. The team heard a voice on their digital recording saying, "Take that," as they heard footsteps. Josh used his medium and psychic skills to get the name of Joanne. He saw her ghost figure in his third eye, and she had blond hair and her hairstyle and attire looked to be from the 1970s. She answered the team's questions through the flashlight that was sitting on the table. David took his mini silver AA Maglite and cranked the handle until the light went out. He set it on the table, and the Ghost Seekers started to ask questions. Len asked, "If you are a worker, please turn on the flashlight." At Len's asking, the flashlight lit up bright. The flashlight went out, and then Josh said, "If this is Joanne, turn on the flashlight." The flashlight came on immediately and was at full bright illumination, leaving the seekers' faces visible in the pitch darkness. The flashlight went out, and Josh started to get a tight feeling in his chest. Josh is also an empath, so spirits tend to send their feelings into his body or attempt to take his life force to power up enough paranormal soul juice to make a mortal view appearance. Len asked, "Are you pleased we want to know you and hear your story?" The flashlight lit up and then quickly went out, as the activity shut off as quick as it had started. The Ghost Seekers gathered their gear and said a closing prayer as they exited the Utica Public Library, satisfied to place the most haunted in Utica stamp on the building. The next time you're in the library, be sure to pay tribute to Ruby's plant, say hello to Joanne and keep quiet and respectful otherwise Patrick may walk up on you with his large ring of ghost world keys.

COLONEL KAST HOUSE

MUDVILLE

The dragon breathes fire across the hallowed ground where the delineation of the living and the dead tread. Jim Skinner is the current owner of the 1798 Colonel Kast house that sits on a hill hidden from the road by deep and thick forest. As you ascend the gravel driveway and round the curve that reveals the house, you feel transported to another time or another place. The vibe and karma throw off the paranormal equilibrium of the most seasoned ghost hunters. On a cold and wet October evening, the Colonel Kast House was visited by the Ghost Seekers of Central New York members Dennis Webster and his wife, Darsy Webster. Jim's beloved wife, Liz, had recently passed, and he felt her spirit was within their loving abode and wanted to have an investigation. When Dennis and Darsy arrived, Jim's pet chickens came out to greet them while he stood on his front porch with a big smile and a wave. Jim is a descendant of the Revolutionary War hero Patrick Henry, whose famous quote, "Give me liberty or give me death," inspired colonists to fight for their freedom and created a free country. Henry was

Colonel Kast House. *Ghost Seekers of CNY.*

Spiritual shaman, Jim Skinner, is the caretaker of the Colonel Kast estate. *Ghost Seekers of CNY.*

an attorney, planter and orator, and his descendant Jim Skinner certainly inherited the verbal skills and gravitas, as he strikes an elegant pose and warm demeanor as he hugs you like a brother the second he meets you. It was still light outside when the Websters arrived, so Jim took them on a tour of the grounds. He described the coyotes that you hear howl in the night yet don't come down the hill and through the forest, as there is a frack in the ground that causes a delineation of energy that Jim described as the breath of the dragon. He says on quiet nights you straddle the border and you will hear the breathing of the dragon. Walking the squishy sod in that area, you feel a certain change in your mood and the energy within the atmosphere. It's hard to describe other than the feel one would have piercing the veil of another dimension.

Jim took Dennis and Darsy through his large barn with slivers of sunlight seeping through the warped cracks of hundred-year-old boards. The barn didn't feel paranormal, but nearby the area felt heavy, as it was a pet cemetery. The animals buried there had their souls leave their bodies, and you could feel their spirits as you walked the ground of their burial. When Jim brought the Ghost Seekers into his house, you could feel the energy of spirits the nanosecond you crossed the threshold. Jim said the house sits on the fairy side of the property, not the dragon side. He said that the house was so old that fifty-eight people had passed within its lifespan. Back during the Revolutionary War, Jim stated that the property adjacent to the house was Tory land, and it hosted both the British and colonists. Jim brought Dennis and Darsy up to the second floor and within the master bedroom described how when his wife, Liz, was alive, they'd wake up and he'd see the ghost of an Oneida Indian woman standing beside the bed looking at them. Liz felt comfortable and not frightened at all as the spirit had been trying to send a message. Jim stated that the house also hosts a male entity and a grumpy girl child ghost who wants the living to play with her. He described his brother living there, but he left when he was on the other second-floor bedroom and woke up to find an entity laying on his chest trying to suck the air out of his mouth.

The team went back downstairs to gather equipment and begin ghost hunting. Jim sat quietly in his living room, sipping a glass of bourbon while the investigation was being conducted, but first he had to say a prayer with Mr. and Mrs. Ghost. They held hands, and Jim whispered a prayer before Dennis and Darsy headed upstairs with their ghost hunting equipment and their open eyes, minds and hearts. The investigators sat in the upstairs bedroom where Jim's brother had his scary haunt, and immediately the devices for

Author Dennis Webster's drawing of dark entity from his dream. *Drawing by Dennis Webster.*

detecting spirits began to trickle on and flick along with the flashlight that was sitting on the bed. Dennis had a dream the night before of the ghost investigation and had seen in this very bedroom a figure cloaked in black with a pointed top. Dennis had awakened and drew a picture of the entity in his dream, and at that moment, he saw the figure in the bedroom. Darsy could not identify the gender of the cloaked entity, with Dennis theorizing it

The dragon's breath emitting from the earth at the Colonel Kast estate. *Ghost Seekers of CNY.*

might not be a human soul but a shadow person. The investigators were overwhelmed and had to go back downstairs to the first floor. They went into a small office where they had felt a presence. All seemed quiet, and Dennis was snapping photographs when one picture showed a massive spirit light surrounding Darsy. The last thing was to go outside in the dark, as Dennis wanted to get pictures of the border of the dragon side of the property. He captured spirits seeping from the ground and rising as if the dragon has dormant beneath the sod snorting out its breath.

The investigation ended with a closing prayer and the Ghost Seekers doing a shot of bourbon with Jim, as he is a considerate host and insisted on tipping a glass of spirits to the spirits. Jim said that the ghosts came alive and were more active after the investigation, as if they had been discovered and might not have liked it. The Colonel Kast house would not be the last time the team would work with Jim, as he invited them to go investigate the Episcopal church in Herkimer, New York. There is no doubt the Colonel Kast house and the surrounding grounds are a magical place of ghosts and dragons, fairies and spirits, with the optimistic and magnetic Jim Skinner as the shamanic ringleader.

EPISCOPAL CHURCH

HERKIMER

Worship and spirits abound beautiful in the place where souls rest in peace yet stir in the restless afterlife. Jim Skinner, poet, orator and man of the word, yet again graced the Ghost Seekers of Central New York with his gentlemanly presence, but this time it was not be his beloved home for the ghost hunt but his place of love and worship at the Episcopal church. The church was built in 1888 and has hosted baptisms, wedding and funerals for over 135 years. A church is a sacred place where people are inspired and feel a connection to

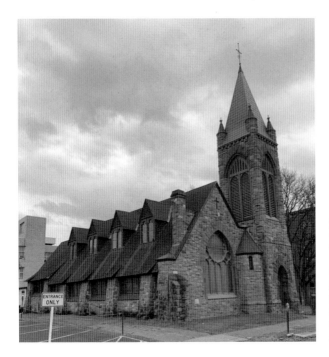

Left: The holy and haunted Episcopal church. *Ghost Seekers of CNY.*

Opposite: Darsy Webster from the Ghost Seekers connecting with the spirits at the Episcopal church with her Ghost Meter. *Ghost Seekers of CNY.*

the afterlife and heaven. Darsy and Dennis Webster investigated along with a guest medium on a cold December Saturday evening. The church and attached rectory were beautiful, and the Websters walked through with Jim as he described the workings of the church. The team settled in and decided to go up to the third floor. At the top of the stairs, there are rooms to the left and right, but the seekers went straight ahead and sat in a room that had extra pew chairs of rough wood, not finished. As the group was talking, the ghost meter in Darsy's hand started to blast full. There was a presence that was curious but wouldn't reveal itself. After a while, it got quiet, and the medium felt that the spirit had left the team, so the gear was picked up and moved down into the second-floor library. It was a small room full of stacked books. The atmosphere and the karma felt airy and light as the team sat on the floor with the handheld devices huddled together in the center. The best way to communicate with ghosts is to chat and ask questions in a respectful and gentle manner. The Ghost Seekers get great results with this low-key style, and it paid off in the library as the group was approached by the same spirit that had been on the third floor. This time it felt comfortable enough to say her name was Maggie. When the medium revealed the name, the ghost hunting meters on the floor all started the chime and illuminate, indicating Maggie was present. The interaction came to a conclusion, so the

96

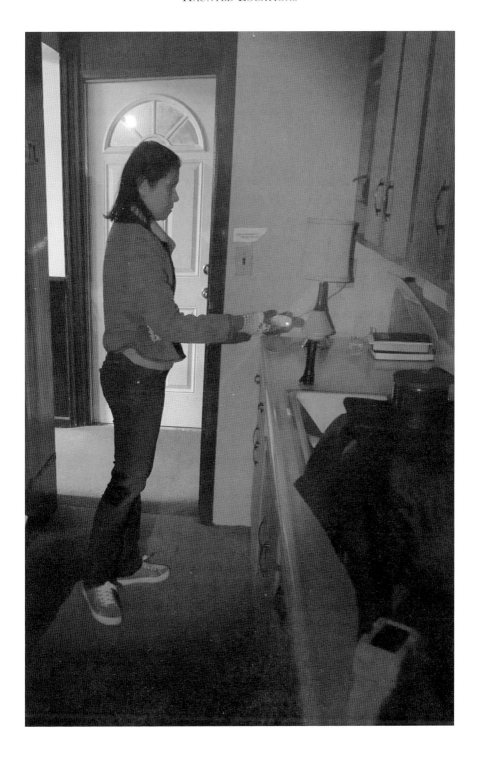

group decided to walk the first floor but not conduct an investigation around the pews and altar.

Out of respect, the seekers steered clear of that area, although it was quite beautiful. The team decided to conduct an electronic voice phenomenon (EVP) session in the back room, where the priests' robes and ceremonial accoutrements were arranged. The team was talking, and the medium put her hands on one of the priest's robes. The ghost meters lit up, and the medium stated she felt a surge of energy from the garment. She pulled her hands away, and everything stopped. Everyone was amazed at this, and after a few quiet moments, the medium wondered if the paranormal spike would happen if she touched the large cross that is carried into the church during service. The medium reached her hands out and didn't touch the cross. She stated she felt nothing. Then she placed her hands on it, and the ghost devices lit up and she stated she was getting the exact same feeling as she had when she touched the robes. The Ghost Seekers decided to end the investigation, as they felt that the spirits of the Episcopal church were content and not wanting to be disturbed so out of respect the team shut off the devices, stored them away, held hands and said a closing prayer thanking the ghosts for the communication and interaction. Maggie never did say what she wanted, but Dennis and Darsy felt that she only wanted to say hello and be acknowledged. Many ghosts are happy in the afterlife and content with their hauntings. When the team spoke to Jim, he agreed and stated that it makes sense the ghosts would be happy in the church, as it was a place of many wonderful moments and he always sensed and embraced the positive karma and mellow juju within the Episcopal church.

1884 SUITER MANSION

HERKIMER

Be wary of the wooden autopsy table in the attic that has become engrained the life juices of the recently departed. This artifact was the most haunted item that the Ghost Seekers of Central New York had ever encountered. The team was invited to investigate the 1884 Suiter Mansion by the Herkimer County Historical Society. The beautiful mansion was built in the Queen Anne style. It housed the office of Dr. Augustus Walter Suiter, who was the secretary of the Herkimer County Medical Society and an expert

The 1884 Suiter Mansion. *Ghost Seekers of CNY.*

pathologist who was used in many murder trials. Dr. Suiter passed away in 1925 at the age of seventy-five, but he left a lasting impact in the medical field and perhaps his ghost remains within the beautiful carved mahogany of his work quarters. The Ghost Seekers were the first paranormal team to ever investigate the mansion and were eager to see what they would encounter within the darkness of the midnight moonlight and under the glow of their paranormal devices. The Ghost Seekers would be represented at the investigation by Bernadette Peck, David Peck, Dennis Webster, Len Bragg, Paranormal Ed Livingston, Helen Clausen and Josh Aust. The entire spiritual-seeking technological arsenal had been brought along, and the team took a good hour setting up the digital cameras on tripods.

The exact locations were selected by Bernadette, Helen and Josh as they walked every square inch of the mansion to use their medium and psychic skillset to identify the hottest paranormal locations. A place deemed to be a dead zone or least likely to host a ghost was chosen as ghost central, where all the cameras were wired into a large flat-screen television. One seeker sits in the command chair, watches the investigation and chronicles any evidence they observed. The seekers gathered in the first-floor library to hold hands and perform their prayer with Bernadette asking the good spirits to come forth and communicate. There were enough investigators on hand to break up into two teams, with one heading up to the attic and the other to go into the basement. The mansion was large enough that the teams wouldn't pick up talking or footsteps of the others, which could be misconstrued as evidence. Dennis decided to sit at ghost central and watch the monitors. The interior lights were extinguished, and the teams went off to their areas with Dennis sitting under the glow of the television. He had to concentrate, as he had six feeds at the same time piping into the television. Before the groups even got to their locations, he observed orbs and spirit lights flowing under the night vision eyes of the positioned video cameras. Dennis then was startled by footsteps behind him. He turned and looked, and nobody was there.

The teams in the attic and basement immediately caught paranormal activity. In the large attic, there are many items stored on behalf of the Herkimer County Historical Society, but one particular item in the back is the wooden autopsy table used by Dr. Suiter. One can only imagine the life juices of the dead bodies examined on this table as their secretions and fluids soaked into the grain and turned a simple wooden table into a device of enormous afterlife energy. Josh had placed his hands on the table, and his entire body lit up with energy reaching out from the other side. Helen placed her hands on the table and had to pull them back as it felt like a red-hot iron stovetop. The team placed their ghost meters and a flashlight on the table and started to ask questions. Paranormal Ed asked if Dr. Suiter was there to turn on the flashlight. It came on bright. It stayed on for several minutes before Len asked Dr. Suiter to please step back and let it shut off and the flashlight went out. During this exchange, the ghost meters kept chiming and going off as if the doctor's ghost were waving his otherworldly hands across them in an orchestral display.

Len was picking up on his night vision camera a multitude of orbs floating and dancing among the Ghost Seekers. The team then asked for a knock to let them know a ghost was present, and two loud knocks were given in reply. Josh and Bernadette returned later to look at the autopsy table; Bernadette placed her hands on it and said a female ghost was lying on it. Josh picked up a name with his third paranormal eye and said, "Rebecca. Is that your name?" At that moment, the flashlight illuminated, and the K2 meter spiked all the way to the top. The basement was creepy, and the team picked up spirits risen from the dead bodies that had been brought through the basement entrance to be autopsied by Dr. Suiter. The entire Ghost Seeker team was down there when they heard footsteps coming down the hall. It was at this

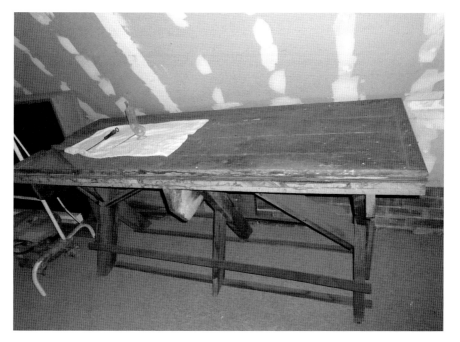

Dr. Suiter's haunted autopsy table. *Ghost Seekers of CNY.*

point that one of the digital cameras sitting on a tripod was hit by an unseen force. On video you can see the video footage shake even though there is nobody near the camera. The team had enough, as Helen felt exhausted and drained and everyone agreed the energy was sapping the members' strength. Everyone was up on the top floor except David and Dennis, who were retrieving the cameras and wires strung into the creepy basement. As David and Dennis got to the top of the basement stairs, they heard the clear and distinct talking of a woman entity. Her voice was sweet and clear from within the inkblot darkness of the basement. David and Dennis looked at each other with stunned expressions, as the lady ghost talking was so clean and out of nowhere that it startled the veteran spirit hunters. It was Rebecca trying to send a message, but sadly the recording devices were picked up and powered down.

The 1884 Suiter Mansion is haunted by the loving Dr. Suiter and the souls of the patients he examined after their departure from our earthly plane, with the main ghost lady the dear Rebecca who wanders the mansion and sleeps on the wooden autopsy table—the most haunted artifact the Ghost Seekers of Central New York had ever encountered.

JUST AN OL' FARM HOUSE
WEST WINFIELD

Your stay will include a warm bed, a serene experience and a ghost guest to share your quarters. Christine Huxtable is the owner and invited Dennis Webster and his wife, Darsy, from the Ghost Seekers of Central New York to come in and see if there were any spirits around. This investigation would be different, as Christine didn't think there were any ghosts haunting her bed-and-breakfast. Even when a place has haunted interactions and many ghost stories doesn't mean a paranormal investigation will yield anything, and on occasion the Ghost Seekers draw a neutral evening where the ghosts stay away. Dennis and Darsy were excited to give it a try, so on a chilly February evening they arrived to the Just an Ol' Farm House with nothing more than a few handheld ghost devices, a digital recorder and a full-spectrum night vision camera. Christine unlocked the place and showed the duo a picture she found during the remodel, as the home was from the nineteenth century.

Bed, breakfast and ghosts at the Just an Ol' Farm House. *Ghost Seekers of CNY.*

Siblings Mina and Dwight ghosts walk the Just an Ol' Farm House. *Courtesy Christine Huxtable.*

The picture was of a brother and sister, Mina and Dwight Purchase, who had lived in the home and were elderly in the photo. Dennis asked Christine why the one side of the house from the exterior looked so different, and she said that the one side was originally built on the property and the small section where the kitchen is had been moved from Connecticut to be placed and attached to the original. Dennis and Darsy thought this was interesting and speculated the moved building could have carried a spirit with it.

The couple were left alone in the dark house and immediately went up to the second-floor bedrooms and began an electronic voice phenomenon (EVP) session in which they asked Mina and Dwight to make an appearance. Things were quiet for a while, and the seekers thought perhaps there wasn't anything in the house after all, until a noise came from the stairs. Something was ascending the stairs. When they looked, there was nobody there. Dennis had left a ghost meter on the kitchen counter, and it started to ring a chime, as it was now detecting a ghost in proximity. The couple walked into the kitchen, and again there was nobody there, when suddenly they heard footsteps on the stairs to the cellar. The door was locked, as the team did not have permission to go in that area of the house, so they went into the comfortable living room and sat in chairs and just watched and said few words. It was at this point that Darsy caught out of the corner of her eye a shadow person in the doorway by the stairs to the second floor. After that, things went quiet and all the spirits seemed to drift away. Christine may not have noticed the ghosts, as Mina and Dwight were very shy and quiet ghosts, and even the ghost hunters barely picked them up.

All places that are haunted have a different aura within them, with some being sad, depressing, scary or outright lively. The Just an Ol' Farm House has a slight hint of the paranormal with shy ghost siblings that may appear. So go and stay the night, and you might just catch a glimpse or hear the soft footsteps of people who loved their house in life and choose to stay there in the afterlife.

1852 WALCOTT FAMILY CRYPT

NEW YORK MILLS

In a cemetery on a hill, there's a place where a family is placed above the ground and their spirits remain guarding the family tomb. The 1852 Walcott family crypt hosts one of the founders of New York Mills. Benjamin Walcott came from Scotland with a bright mind and hard work ethic. He founded the gristmill and the first textile factory in what would become a solid working-class community. It was a fitting tribute to Benjamin Walcott to have a beautiful final resting place in a community that he gave his heart and soul to. The Ghost Seekers of Central New York have always been attracted to cemeteries and graveyards. Dennis was going to visit a friend

in New York Mills when he drove past a small cemetery that he had no clue had been in that particular location. He felt drawn to the place, as his grandfather was born in the town, so he felt that there were probably friends he had known buried in there. He was looking around with respect, admiring the markers, when he noticed a crypt on the far corner that called to him. He walked over, and the inside stone door was wide open, and the outside iron gate was unlocked and slightly ajar. The curiosity of being a paranormal investigator got the best of him, and he stepped inside. His entire body rippled with goosebumps as he noticed one of the inside coffin resting places was an open cavity and the casket was missing. Dennis said a prayer for the missing person and stepped backward out of the crypt. He closed the doors and looked at the engraving that was at the top, and it said, "Walcott Family 1852." Dennis left and called Bernadette Peck to come back and help say a prayer, for the spirits were restless inside the crypt. When they arrived the next day, the doors were closed and locked. They said a few kind words for the spirits of the Walcott family to rest in peace.

Opposite, top: View from inside the Walcott family crypt. *Ghost Seekers of CNY.*

Opposite, bottom: Inside the Walcott family crypt. *Ghost Seekers of CNY.*

Above: Walcott family crypt. *Ghost Seekers of CNY.*

ORCHARD HALL
SAUQUOIT

A banquet hall delights the ghost of the original owner who oversees all who embrace the food and the warm spirits within the grand Orchard Hall. The Butler family built and named the building Butler Hall, and that name remained its moniker until 1920, when a new owner renamed it Orchard Hall in tribute to the apple orchard that sat behind the pillar-adorned mansion. Dr. George Armstrong ran it as a speakeasy in 1932, with illegal bottles of booze lowered out of the second-floor windows on ropes in order to be hidden in the apple orchard when the law came to inspect and bust Dr. Armstrong's establishment for breaking the laws of Prohibition. Orchard Hall became a private residence until 1957, when it ran as a restaurant and bowling alley. Gary and Sharon Puleo have owned Orchard Hall for the past thirty years and have a wealth of ghost interaction and tales of the spooky that earns the hall a reputation as a pleasantly haunted establishment. The Ghost Seekers of Central New York were represented by Dennis Webster and Darsy Webster, as they were invited by the Puleos to a sit-down interview to go over their haunted occurrences and give a walking tour to point out the ghost hot spots.

The outside of Orchard Hall is a marvel of antique beauty, as it pops from Oneida Street when you drive by. Passersby cannot help but stop and stare at the grand white mansion that's welcomed family, friends and patrons for a long time. The Ghost Seekers were aware of the haunted legend of Orchard Hall, and it was on their wish list of haunted places where they'd love to conduct a paranormal investigation. The lady ghost who haunts the upper floors and stairs is Julia. Dennis and Darsy walked into the front door and heard the sweet voice from at the top of the stairs saying she'd be right down. It was the owner, Sharon, who lives on the second floor with her husband. Dennis had not said anything to Darsy about the legend of Julia or any stories about the place, as he wanted her to walk in there cold with no preconceived spookiness planted in her hypothalamus. Dennis had his pad and pen in order to scribe down the ghost stories while Darsy was armed with nothing but a ghost meter to check the electromagnetism. The unnatural spike of magnetic fields can sometimes indicate a ghost is present. Darsy was looking down the hallway toward the back dining room and froze. Dennis knew by her reaction that she had seen something but remained silent until she spoke. "I saw a female ghost," said Darsy, who described her

Above: The legendary haunted Orchard Hall. *Ghost Seekers of CNY.*

Right: Paranormal investigator Darsy Webster looking for Julia the ghost inside the grand Orchard Hall. *Ghost Seekers of CNY.*

as a woman with a long dress in a late 1800s style with dark brown hair that was pinned up into a Victorian-style coiffure worn by elegant ladies. The lady ghost disappeared, and the ghost meter started to blast its signal as if she went invisible and bolted past the seekers.

Gary and Sharon came down the stairs and introduced themselves and walked the team into the dining room, where everyone sat at a round table and discussed ghosts. Darsy didn't say anything about Julia, as she wanted to hear the Puleos talk of what had happened at Orchard Hall. Gary started out by saying he wasn't sure if he believed in this stuff, but he had a lot of great stories. There had been many people who had seen the ghost of Julia in the upstairs bedroom, and Gary's cousin went up there and saw the same entity. Gary and Sharon smiled when they told the story of their grandson JP. When JP was three years old, he was standing at the bottom of the stairs looking up and staring in silence. When asked what he was doing, JP said he was looking at the little girl sitting at the top of the steps. The adults looked, and nobody was there. Decades ago, Orchard Hall was host to a man who played the piano and his wife, who was a singer. The couple commuted from Lake George, but one winter weekend the storm was so intense that they asked to stay in the empty upstairs room. The couple also had their two dogs with them. Gary stopped by early the next morning, and they were gone. The next week when they came back, the lady singer said they had left because of the ghost. They were hunkered down in bed when they heard footsteps coming to their bedroom door; the door opened, and there was nobody there. The door then shut with more footsteps, and the dogs started to bark. The couple packed up their belongings and their pups and fled. Not long after that, the lady singer misplaced the datebook that she planned everything in. She had it come up missing during their performance and thought it was gone until the next week they came back, and it was sitting on the floor next to her microphone stand.

Gary and Sharon did have one amazing haunted photo that someone had sent them from a wedding reception that had taken place at Orchard Hall in the 1970s. The wedding party was standing in a row up the inside stairs, and at the top was an all-white figure of a ghost posing with the bride, groom and wedding party. For years, the Puleos had that framed picture on the wall in the bar. One day it simply disappeared. The theory is that either a paranormal enthusiast stole it, or Julia took it off the wall and hid it away. Dennis told Gary someday he may be remodeling and find it tucked inside a wall. The haunting of Orchard Hall remains consistent to this day. Gary has occasions where he leaves a room and the lights are off only to come back on; one time he was working on a piece of the bowling alley equipment and it mysteriously shut off. He tried everything to get the power back on and finally realized something had turned the power switch to the off position. Sharon said the downstairs ladies' room has ghost interactions all the time, with the scariest one coming from a lady who was in a stall, sitting on the toilet with the stall door shut. Suddenly, the stall door opened and a hand of a lady wearing a black velvet glove reached in and tried to grab her. The lady screamed, jumped up and quickly opened the stall door, and nobody was there. One time two ladies were sitting at the bar enjoying a frosty beverage and were saying there was no such thing as ghosts. They were laughing and mocking the haunting of Orchard Hall until a piece fell from the ceiling light and landed on the bar exactly in the middle of where they were sitting.

The paranormal activity continued even when Gary and Sharon moved into the upstairs that had been vacant for close to their thirty-year ownership. They have a small television upstairs that comes on all by itself and refuses to be turned off with the remote. Gary will unplug it as the only way to shut it off. On other occasions, the television is just fine and the remote works no problem. This television was at their old house and never behaved in this manner. One time Sharon and Gary came back from running errands, and their next-door neighbor was standing there with a look of shock on her face. She told the Puleos that she had just waved to Gary, as she saw a man looking out of the second-floor window. The house was locked, and there was nobody inside. After all the stories, Dennis and Darsy walked the upstairs, with Dennis getting butterflies in his stomach, and Darsy had the ghost meter go off as soon as they walked into the room where everyone claims to see Julia. They then went downstairs, and when the group passed by the ladies' bathroom, the ghost meter pegged where it had not chimed earlier. It was at this time that Darsy explained the woman ghost she had seen earlier. Sharon smiled and said, "That's Julia." Gary then brought the Ghost Seekers into a side room that had historic pictures all over the wall with an old photo of Orchard Hall, and on it was the description of Butler Hall, the original name. Sharon then mentioned how in the Clayville cemetery somebody had found the grave of a Julia Butler. Dennis and Darsy smiled and together said "Wow," as that had to be the resting place of the body of the woman who is eternally haunting the glorious Orchard Hall.

NOTE: The following haunted location is not part of the Central New York area but in the New York State Capitol region. This location was visited by the author, who stayed overnight, walked the building with a psychic and felt the haunted bed-and-breakfast deserved to be known.

GARDNER FARM INN

TROY

Faceless paintings adorn the walls, and fascinating, creepy, eclectic and cool decorations slather every corner of the graceful and beautifully haunted Gardner Farm Inn. Dennis Webster from the Ghost Seekers of Central New York stayed at the inn years ago and felt it was haunted; that time, he stayed in the John Waters room. During that night, he heard voices in his room, and the entire place gave off a paranormal bouquet. He said nothing at that time but always wanted to return, as the owner, John, was a marvelous host and the bed-and-breakfast unique and welcoming. John agreed to allow Dennis and his fellow member of the Ghost Seekers Darsy Webster to come and stay and discuss his tales of the spooky that had occurred at the Gardner Farm Inn. The building was built in two centuries, with the front part of the colonial structure dating to 1790 and the back part added on in 1870. Altogether, the inn is five thousand square feet with many rooms and baths. The inn spent most of its existence as a private home. The original portion was built by Asa and Helen Gardner, who were farmers, but they must've been successful, as their homestead was befitting royalty and those who flaunt their success. The high ceilings, elaborate hardwood molding and complex decorative hardwood floors are a marvel to behold.

Dennis and Darsy arrived to talk ghosts of the inn with John and brought along Dennis's son Jakob Webster. Dennis reached out to two mediums, Irene Crewell and Gina Smith, to come to the discussion and walk of the Gardner Farm Inn. The ladies are highly sought after by paranormal investigative teams, as both have years of experience in connecting with spirits. On a crisp clear January evening, the group descended on the Gardner Farm Inn. John described how the inn was owned by an agency that took care of the developmentally disabled for thirty years before emptying the building and putting it up for sale. John said that during the Civil War the inn was a stop on the Underground Railroad. John purchased the building and had to remodel to make it up to a high-quality standard so he could accept guests, as his dream was to open and run his own bed-and-breakfast. He's sensitive to spirits and felt there were ghosts, as he kept hearing things while alone. He contacted a medium he referred to as Margaret, who walked into the building and said she saw that there was a female ghost that was taking care of four child ghosts. They were there before her, but she decided to stay to watch over them. There was another

Above: The wonderful phantasmagorical Gardner Farm Inn. *Ghost Seekers of CNY.*

Left: The charming and enigmatic owner of the Gardner Farm Inn, John Hughes, on safari. *Courtesy Gardener Farm Inn.*

Left to right: John Hughes, Gina Smith, Irene Crewell and Darsy Webster talk to the lady ghost of the Gardner Farm Inn. *Ghost Seekers of CNY.*

adult female ghost, but she was startled to realize Margaret could see her and disappeared. John had curtains torn down when nobody was there, and the first night he had overnight guests, the ghosts were playful and active all night long, as if they were having an otherworldly celebration of having mortal humans within the bosom on their beloved homestead. Over the years, many guests saw the regal lady ghost. One night, John had an artist and his wife stay in the John Waters room, and in the morning, they said they had seen the children ghosts. The couple was in bed late at night and looked up to see the children ghosts standing there looking at them. The children then walked away without saying anything.

John had started giving the group the tour when Irene felt her back was on fire, that a man entity was trying to channel into her. She took Dennis into the kitchen, where he ran the digital recorder and watched as Irene moved him on. He wanted to leave the Gardner Farm Inn and told Irene his name was John. Come to find out that a previous owner was John Sampson who had bought the farm in 1830. He had tragedy in the house, as his first wife and child died in the home. He then remarried and had two more children but then suddenly died, leaving his widow and young children to tend to the

Faceless painting at Gardner Farm Inn. *Ghost Seekers of CNY.*

farm alone. Gina had a vision of a hiding place that melded perfectly with the Underground Railroad usage. She also had a vision of a young man who would ride a horse past the windows and look in to play a prank. It was later in the evening when Irene saw a young male ghost peeking in the kitchen window from the porch.

The walkthrough went into the Jean Harlow room on the first floor. The ghost meters started to blast full, especially the one in Darsy's hand. Gina had the Mel Meter, and it went from a 0.0 up to a 3.4. Irene asked Darsy if she was seeing something, as she sensed something going on with her, and Darsy said she saw a female ghost with short black hair, wearing an elegant dress and watching them. The group was joined by Jakob Webster, who quietly and curiously watched the happenings. It was at this time that Gina and Dennis both witnessed a small pillow on a chair get picked up and set down. Jakob asked his father later what the big deal was, a cushion moved, but he was silent when Dennis explained it was picked up then set down by a ghost. It was at this point that Irene said she was getting the female name of Catherine. John stated that was his mother's name. Gina stated her face was very hot, but the rest of her body was cold. John then took the team into the basement, where Gina and Irene stopped at a dusty chandelier sitting in a box. It was beautiful but unhung. The mediums placed their hands on the chandelier and told John that the owner was upset about where it was and she wanted him to hang it up. John smiled and said that his good friend had brought it over to the United States from France on a steamship and she would absolutely say to him to hang it and not leave it in the basement.

Gina felt compelled to go toward the basement cistern. She stood in silence as she felt the ghosts of the basement trying to tell her something. She asked John if anybody had ever been buried in it, and he said he didn't know. The group then went to the corner John said gave him creepy feelings. Irene and Gina said a few words to try to move on whatever was there. The group decided to go to the second floor, walked into the Josephine Baker room and felt it was warm and inviting, but the entire team felt uneasy in the library, as it had many religious artifacts on the walls. It was a different vibe and karma but nothing bad or evil, just different. John's beautiful bed-and-breakfast is filled to the brim with amazing antiques from all over the world, and Irene and Gina said some ghosts could be attached or come through the portal by the front door, become enamored with the décor and decide to stay. Dennis was infatuated with the faceless paintings that John had hanging in the hallway and up the back stairs to the second floor. He felt they were a long-ago tribute to the spirits that can sometimes appear without definition or a face. The ghost walk ended, and John made a marvelous dinner of roast pork loin, tossed salad and caramelized carrots served with white and red wine.

The group all discussed the wonderful spirit and positive karma in the Gardner Farm Inn and that John was the perfect owner and host, as it was obvious the ghosts loved him as much as his guests. Irene and Gina were done with their medium work and left with a big hug to the group, satisfied they had the pleasure of walking a pleasant haunted inn. Dennis and Darsy were staying in the Josephine Baker room, and Jakob was staying in the small room at the end of the second-floor hall. In the morning, Darsy said she was awake at 3:00 a.m. and heard a female and a child ghost talking next to her side of the bed. Jakob said that he was awake at 4:00 a.m. and decided to walk the house with his cellphone flashlight illuminated. When he walked into the Jean Harlow room on the first floor, the light on his phone went out. He said that had never happened before. The skeptic was a believer after all he had seen and heard. The Gardner Farm Inn is a unique and warm place to stay where you'll get great company in the host John and a tasty breakfast along with a warm and inviting room. Just be prepared for your stay to include ghosts and Catherine the sweet spiritual lady of the house, who is spending the afterlife watching over the child spirits; the amazing smiling owner, John Hughes; and you.

BEST OF THE REST

The following are additional haunted locations within Central New York. This is not every location with ghost activity, as new ones come to the attention of the Ghost Seekers every week. These are haunted locations known by the seekers.

BEARDSLEE CASTLE

A nationally known haunted castle that features a basement area with ghosts that interact with diners. The Ghost Seekers of Central New York investigated the castle and picked up an entity moving a chair across the dungeon basement floor.

RUTGER MANSION NO. 1

The Rutger No. 1 mansion or "Munn's Castle" in Utica has hosted ghosts in the over one hundred years of its existence. The former grand mansion now sits occupied only by the spirits of the dead as it goes through a renovation by the Landmark Society of Utica.

PLAYERS OF UTICA

Built on top of a destructed church, this playhouse features performances by ghosts. Visitors and performers have witnessed spirits on stage, in the dressing room and greeting visitors at the door. Even spirits of the afterlife wish to perform.

FOREST HILL CEMETERY

More dead are under the ground at this haunted cemetery than are alive in the city of Utica. A place where the ghosts rise to walk among the living. Caretakers have seen the figure of a ghostly man walking his ghost beagles at the top of the cemetery among the grove of trees. This haunted and serene beauty is among the most beautiful resting places in America.

NYS LUNATIC ASYLUM AT UTICA "OLD MAIN"

The NYS Lunatic Asylum at Utica "Old Main" hosts the sad spirits of those who were tormented with mental affliction. Ghost roam the empty halls from the 1843 structure whose Greek Doric columns hold fast the spirits of the sadly departed patients.

HULBERT HOUSE

Wayne the Civil War ghost walks the halls of this Boonville establishment. The Hulbert House was a waystation for young men being transported from the north country to fight their brothers in the Civil War.

HERKIMER COUNTY COURTHOUSE

Ghosts of prosecutors and those sentenced walk the halls of justice in Herkimer. The ghost of a former prosecutor has been seen walking the halls of the courthouse, and the chambers abound with the ghosts of criminal trial spectators and jurors.

Molly MacKinnon Mansion

The grand staircase has Molly's ghost descending to greet the living in this Utica building of beauty. Caretakers of the mansion have witnessed Molly's ghost dancing in the ballroom and walking the halls and staircase in this grand dame of Utica's historic buildings.

Newport Masonic Temple

The grumpy spirits of dead brothers walk the floors of this haunted temple. This haunted brotherhood beauty sits across from the West Canada Creek and hosts the ghosts of the men who dedicated their earthly lives to serving mankind.

Oriskany Battlefield

The spirits of dead brave patriots walk the hallowed ground where they gave their lives for freedom. The Oneida Indians and the Tryon County Militia engaged in a bloody Revolutionary War battle against Loyalists in Oriskany. The ghosts of dead soldiers walk the battlefield for all eternity.

1834 Herkimer County Jail

The ghosts of those hanged and sentenced to death linger in the cells and drift along the entrances. The ghosts of killers Chester Gillette and Roxy Druse walk the jail and interact with the mortality of the living. The basement cells and metal tables entice the ghosts to bang and clang in order to scare the living.

Russia Union Church

The church and adjacent schoolhouse are overstuffed with spirits who are curious and interact with the living. The second floor of the church features a dark cloaked figure who is grumpy and doesn't interact well with visitors. The schoolhouse features a child entity who has been seen running the grounds and rolling balls at visitors.

HISTORY OF GHOST HUNTING

Human beings have been fascinated with the spirits of the dead since the dawn of Promethius delivering fire down from the gods. We are the only creatures on earth who are aware of our mortality and the knowledge of a soul fire energy that exists inside each and every one of us. Many cultures embrace and provide tribute and offerings to the ancestors who are the ghosts of loved ones and people who have departed our mortal realm for the afterlife. The history of the belief in ghosts in the United States of America traces its roots back to England, where in the twelfth century legends of "revenants" abounded. These were the dead who rose from the grave and walked around. The first recorded ghost story in England was written by a fourteenth century monk who lived in a monastery in Byland. He was told a story by a frightened man who had been walking down a road at night when a ghost horse appeared. The man tried to run and was chased by this spirit when it got in front of him and turned into a glowing haystack. The man fell on his knees and prayed to God. The haystack suddenly took the form of a peasant man, who sent a verbal wish upon the mortal man to carry a sack of goods across a bridge. Shakespeare wrote about a ghost in his 1603 play *Hamlet*. Ghost legends existed in the early United States, but the Puritans tamped down anybody wishing to bring forth their encounters. It wouldn't be until 1848 that ghosts would hit the mainstream and became the fascination of the entire United States. In a little hut in Hydesville, New York, lived the young Fox sisters, who claimed they could communicate with ghosts and get them to knock and rap answers to their questions. The Fox sisters launched the spiritualism movement, which birthed séances and attempted communication with the dead.

Mary Todd Lincoln held a séance in the White House when she was trying to connect with her deceased son Willie. The Fox sisters eventually admitted they had committed a hoax, yet their popularity launched psychics, mediums and séances in all corners of the country. In the 1880s, a group of scientists and philosophers grouped together and created the Society for Psychical Research (SPR) by using scientific equipment and methods to speak to the deceased. This was the first time science melded with the paranormal mind to attempt to deliver quantitative results to prove the existence of ghosts. Thomas Edison invented a ghost phone that he claimed would allow a loved one to speak to their dead relatives. Ghost photos by William Hope fascinated the world in the early twentieth century and have been debunked by modern scientists, yet the public hold on ghosts stayed solid.

Top: The Fox sisters who started the spiritualism movement in the nineteenth century. *Public domain.*

Bottom: One of William Hope's ghost photos that were all the rage in the early twentieth century. *Public domain.*

The populace moved on to UFOs for the mid-twentieth century until Ed and Lorraine Warren of *The Conjuring* and *The Amityville Horror* brought ghost hunting back to the forefront. Science advanced in the early 1980s with the creation of the Spontaneous Psychophysical Incident Data Electronic Recorder (SPIDER) by Tony Cornell. This device could record ghosts if they entered into a designated area. The movie *Ghostbusters* debuted in 1984 and throw ghost hunting into the realm of popularity with the characters' use of science and gadgets. This would inspire many people to ghost hunt and form their own ghost hunting teams, with the most popular being the TAPS team starring in the television show *Ghost Hunters*. At this time, teams hunting spirits could easily obtain equipment like the Mel Meter,

Ovilus, night vision cameras, full spectrum cameras, digital recorders and many more to assist in the field. Today, teams abound, and ghost hunting will continue into our future. Perhaps there will be a device that will once and for all prove the existence of ghosts and allow the living to speak to their long-departed loved ones.

BIBLIOGRAPHY

Bentley, Mabel L. *Facts about the Verona Beach Area*. N.p., 1967.

Brae Loch Inn. www.braelochinn.com.

Brown, Jennings. "Proton Packs and Teddy Bears: The Pseudoscientific History of Ghost Hunting Gadgets." *Popular Mechanics*, October 2016. www.popularmechanics.com.

Encyclopædia Britannica. "Roscoe Conkling American Politician." www.britannica.com.

Fort Schuyler Club. "History." http://fortschuylerclub.com.

Grimes, David Robert. "Science of the Séance: Why Speaking to Spirits Is Talking to Yourself." *The Guardian*, October 30, 2015. https://www.theguardian.com.

Haunted History Trail of New York State. "Shoppes at the Finish Line." http://hauntedhistorytrail.com.

Ilion Free Public Library. http://ilionlibrary.org.

New York Mills Public Library, "Story of a Village." www.newyorkmillslibrary.org.

North Carolina Ghosts. "A Brief History of Ghosts." www.northcarolinaghosts.com.

Observer-Dispatch. "Whitesboro Historical Museum Gets New Home." June 16, 2016.

The Rome Capitol Theatre. www.romecapitol.com.

Shechan, Megan. "Syracuse Eats: Angry Garlic of Baldwinsville." *Syracuse Woman Magazine*, June 2019.

The Stanley Theatre. www.thestanley.org.
Sylvan Beach. "History of Sylvan Beach." https://sylvanbeachny.com.
Town of Westernville History. http://townofwestern-ny.org.
Utica Public Library. www.uticapubliclibrary.org.

About the Author

Photo by Karl Ermisch.

Dennis Webster is a ghost hunter and paranormal investigator with the Ghost Seekers of Central New York. He has walked haunted churches, theaters, temples and graveyards. He's the published author of *Haunted Adirondacks*, *Haunted Utica*, *Haunted Old Forge* and *Haunted Mohawk Valley*. He's written books on true crime and lunatic asylums. He has a Bachelor of Science degree from Utica University and a Master of Business Administration (MBA) degree from the State University of New York Polytechnic. He can be reached by email at denniswbstr@gmail.com.

FREE eBOOK OFFER

Scan the QR code below, enter your e-mail address and get our original Haunted America compilation eBook delivered straight to your inbox for free.

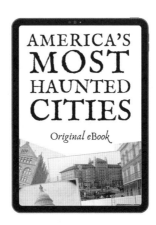

ABOUT THE BOOK

Every city, town, parish, community and school has their own paranormal history. Whether they are spirits caught in the Bardo, ancestors checking on their descendants, restless souls sending a message or simply spectral troublemakers, ghosts have been part of the human tradition from the beginning of time.

In this book, we feature a collection of stories from five of America's most haunted cities: Baltimore, Chicago, Galveston, New Orleans and Washington, D.C.